MY SYSTEM

by J.P. Müller

JP Muller proposes his system as an alternative to Eugene Sandow's method.
Rather than focusing on a "bodybuilding" method he offers a system based on health and practicality.

CONTENT

BOOK I: MY SYSTEM

PREFACE

The Exercises called "My System" were originally selected and composed for the purpose of keeping my comrades of the Copenhagen Rowing Club and myself it during the "off" season, as regular rowing practice is not possible during winter in Denmark.

Up to this time, the manuals of physical culture in vogue were published with the main object of selling some apparatus (spring dumbbells, chest-expanders, etc,). On the title page were usually displayed as "authors" the names of famous stage performers, whose biceps or triceps were their chief credentials.

Seeing the splendid results in general health and fitness of my exercises without apparatus, my friends urged me to let them be published. The first Danish edition appeared in 1904 and had an immediate success ; several reprints had to be issued, even in the first few months, and the fame of the little book rapidly spread to other countries.

The subsequent demand for the book has been so great that it has been translated into 24 languages, the sales numbering millions of copies. One of the main causes of this phenomenal success has been the general and generous support from members of the Medical Profession all over the world. In some countries, Italy, Portugal and Spain, the book and its companion volumes have even been translated by Doctors of Medicine, who asked me for permission to introduce "My System" amongst their countrymen. These doctors [respectively. Dr. Alessandro Clerici, Dr, Atdisson Ferreira, and Dr. Alberto Conradi) put their full names on the title pages and wrote long eulogistic prefaces.

It was the scientific merits of "My System" its recognition of the fundamental importance of the establishment of general health in all the vital, organic functions, rather than in the development of merely muscular strength, which commanded the immediate approval of the Medical Profession,

The endorsement of the " System " by the leading medical men of Europe, the constant comments and favourable analytic reviews in the Continental medical Press, the publicity given to it at several Medical Congresses, where it formed the subject of addresses and debates, and last but not least, the references to it in numerous medical works published by well-known Continental savants, speedily commended it to British physicians, who were only too ready to investigate a physical culture system so free from the taint of commercialism, and which recognised as essential the importance of medical advice in carrying out the instructions.

From 1905 to 1912 I spent my time mainly in travelling in all the countries of Europe, giving lectures and demonstrations ; but in 1912 I gave way to the persuasions of English friends and settled in London, where " The Muller Institute " was established at 45 Dover Street.

The aim of my first editions was first of all to show how the fairly healthy, average person could keep fit, fortify health and stamina and increase physical and mental efficiency. But as so many doctors recommended the book to chronic sufferers and placed it in the hands of their patients, it became more and more evident that this " System " also formed a splendid means of curing several chronic ailments.

This fact has been further proved in the last nine years, during which period a steadily increasing number of doctors have sent their patients to be treated at the Institute. The list of specialists and medical practitioners in London and the suburbs who recommend my exercises to their clients now numbers over 500, of whom 20 are titled, and many Fellows of the Royal College of Physicians and of the Royal College of Surgeons. Several of these doctors have had personal instruction at the Institute for the benefit of their own health, and a number have sent members of their own family.

Several thousand persons have been instructed and treated at the Muller Institute, or by special course sent by post. But the millions, the great mass of the population of the whole Empire are, of course, lacking the opportunity or the means of securing such personal or special attention.

I AM, THEREFORE, PUBLISHING THIS NEW EDITION IN ORDER TO GIVE EVERYBODY IN THE WORLD AN OPPORTUNITY OF BENEFITING BY ALL THE VALUABLE EXPERIENCE GAINED DURING RECENT YEARS.

In former editions only a strenuous form or degree of each exercise was fully described. It was often, therefore, rather risky for patients to do them on their own account, and it was difficult for their medical advisers to explain to them how the same exercises could be done in milder forms. Now, in this new edition, the very easiest degrees or quite simple preliminary movements of every exercise axe described in full detail and profusely illustrated. It is further explained which exercises are best for most Common chronic diseases or bodily disabilities. The task of the medical adviser who prescribes my exercises is consequently much easier, and his prescriptions are sure to have still more beneficial results than formerly.

People not suffering from any ailment, but who are of advanced age or unaccustomed to physical exercise, can study this new edition, and by following the exercise programme for beginners laid down on page 52, learn the whole " System " properly and correctly.

In the description of each exercise I have warned against every possible mistake which otherwise might have disappointed the hope of deriving good and speedv benefits.

Since the patronage of H.R.H. the Prince of Wales was graciously granted for my works and books and not for institutes, I am no more connected with this line of business.

J.P MULLER

HEALTH VERSUS ILLNESS

Why be Weakly?

It has often surprised me that so many people are content to be weak and ill, when in reality there is only a slight effort required on their part for them to grow sound and well. and remain so. But certainly there is a general impression abroad that illness and delicacy are things that must be : a necessary evil.

There are, however, people of both sexes who actually make a parade of their ailments and what they consider to be their " pale and interesting " appearance, under the impression that pallid, sickly looks are an infallible index of an apathetic and soulful nature. Other Signs of ill-health and weakness, such as premature baldness or corpulency, are regarded by many as marks of dignity-and distinction—the same false dignity which forbids people, for instance, to indulge in so healthy and beneficial an exercise as running.

Some of our men of letters have caused incalculable mischief in youth by systematically extolling, both by their example and in their writings, a mixture of exclusively intellectual culture physical decadence, and mental morbidity, Fortunately there are now signs that their influence is on the wane, so that we who work for the advancement of physical culture, and the moral culture which is its natural result, may also hope for a hearing ; I shall, therefore, henceforward ignore the fact that delicacy of health or appearance is regarded in certain circles as an attribute worth striving for.

Illness is not by any means a thing that one need submit to blindly. Even hereditary tendencies may be successfully combated, and the constitutional inclination held in check.

Antiquated modes of thought are chiefly responsible for the prevailing wrong point of view Common adages such as "Illness is Everyone's Master !" have made good folk sit down with their hands in their laps, and submit to anything. Many indeed even defy the laws of Nature and the decrees of Hygiene, arguing " We shall get ill in any case, so let us enjoy ourselves as long as we can ; we need not be afraid that our folly and indolence will arouse contempt ; on the contrary, we shall be objects of gratifying sympathy to the many who think as we do."

If people only knew how much more, how much better and how much longer they can enjoy life if, instead of being controlled by a weakly body, they have a strong and healthy one at their command !

Illness is generally One's Own Fault

Even Hippocrates the celebrated physician of olden times, understood that illness is not a bolt from the blue, but is rather the result al a series of daily small transgressions, which pile themselves up little by little until they burst like a thunder-cloud over the heads of the foolish.

Many people ruin their own health by committing such deadly hygienic sins as always going about in a tight-laced corset and with too high heels, or filling themselves every day with strong drink and too rich and indigestible food, and inhaling and absorbing into their blood, day and night, poisonous gases, which they, and others in the same room, have exhaled and exuded. Many others fall ill through sins of omission. He who does not take care of his body, neglects it, and thereby sins against Nature ; she knows no forgiveness of sins, but revenges herself with mathematical certainty. If you do not take a bath and some all-round exercise daily [a walk does not merit this description), and do not see that you have from seven to eight hours sleep at night, regularly, it is your own fault if you are ill, for you have troubled neither to get rid of the poisonous matter which is generated in your own body, nor to render the latter capable of resisting infection from without. It would consequently be absolutely logical to regard it as a species of fraud for persons, for example, who hold business or official appointments, to live in direct opposition to the simplest rules of health, with the result that they are obliged to lie up every year for a longer or shorter period, and entail extra expense upon their employer, the State, or the Municipality, as the case may be, and similarly, if a man be delicate and yet, for the sake of additional profit, saddle himself with more sedentary brain-work, instead of making use of the leisure which his regular daily head-work leaves in order to fortify his health.

Quite recently a man declared in a death announcement that the Government had killed his second child, because there were still not establishments enough for the treatment of poor tuberculosis patients ! There may be some truth in the thought, but the State ought in return to have the right to prohibit keeping the sunniest room for show, sleeping at right with closed windows and without urgent necessity, leading an unhealthy life generally.

We, who make a serious effort to be well, have to watch people committing sins against Hygiene which are simply enough to make one's hair stand on end, without daring, even unobstrusively, to suggest that they should stop. They would certainly retort; "What business is it of yours. Sir ?" Yes, and we have to bear the heavy cost of those places of refuge—hospitals and lunatic asylums—for such "sinners" and their offspring.

Do not point to this man or the other who, despite the fact that he pays no heed to his bodily health, is to all appearance well. His time will come sooner or later. He may possibly be fortunate enough to escape infection, but he will never attain the feeling of exuberant health that a rational care of the body produces. He does not live, he only vegetates. He has wasted the stock of vitality that he may possibly have inherited from healthy parents. His children will be so much the weaker.

So let us not close our eyes, but rather hold up to the light the fact that practically all illness and delicacy Is something for which, we have to thank ourselves, or at any race our parents, and let us begin as soon as possible to shake off this yoke of illness, that our children may not when they are grown up, be able to call us to account for allowing them, and even helping them, to neglect their lungs and limbs, and ruin their teeth and stomachs.

What Ought we to Do ?

That I have already pointed out. Make use of fresh air and clean water ; let the sun shine upon you, and do not let a day pass without every muscle and every organ in your body being set in brisk motion, even if only for a short time. Stagnation in this case, as everywhere else in Nature, is abnormal and leads to drooping and untimely death. Motion is life, increases and maintains vitality up to life's normally late limit.

If illness, pursuant to the law of cause and effect, be as a rule our own fault, we ourselves, on the other hand, can secure the contrary blessings, namely, Health and Beauty. Everyone is the architect of his own happiness ; but happiness depends on health, and not on dignities or power, or on a pile of money inherited or scraped together. The business man who, because he has been earning a fortune, has not been able to find tune to take care of his health, has doubtless, in many good people's opinion, behaved in an exceedingly sensible manner. But when he comes to reap "the fruits," as they are so well called, of his breathless drudgery, only one of the two following alternatives awaits him: either to die of it all prematurely or to pass the rest of his life in a state of constant annoyance because his poor ill-treated body does not allow him to enjoy life, but compels him to spend his money on specialists or expensive cures, Tacitus of old writes: "When a man has attained the age of 30, he is either an idiot or his own doctor." If we put "hygienic adviser" in the place of "doctor," this still holds good. There may of course be cases in which it is judicious to take medicine oneself, or humane to give it to others, but this is an exception and must not become a rule. And in any case everyone ought to know that each time he takes even the smallest dose he increases his distance from the ideal of health, whereas he draws nearer to it by conquering illness without the use of medicine—should he happen to have been too late in starting to harden himself against illness. In the same way one ought not always to fly to the doctor for medicine the moment one feels a trifle unwell. (Of course, I am not speaking here about acute illnesses. If you get a serious cold or fever, go to bed at once and send for your doctor. You will then recover in a few days, whereas it may take several weeks if you try to ignore the fever.) One should search in one's own bosom and ask:

"Why am I not so strong and well as I should like to be ?"

The sensible man is obliged to reply:

"I do not trouble to fortify my body in a natural manner; but I will begin to do so now, and thus avoid disease."

If it be stupid to stuff oneself with medicine on the slightest provocation it is simply idiocy to let oneself be led by the nose by all the mercenary, but unscrupulous and irresponsible, business people who through advertisements, with in part, spurious references, prey upon the blind credulity of the public. There does not exist any hocus-pocus, witchcraft, magic cure, or nostrum (such as Gout Tablets, Electric Belts, Elixir of Life, Liver Pills, Nerve Tonics, or whatever the trash may be called) that is able to give people health. The Philosopher's Stone is nothing of that sort ; it is simply and solely a healthy mode of life. It is incomprehensible that so straightforward a thing should present difficulties to so many, even among educated and enlightened people. I can only imagine one reason for it —indolence. Of course it is less trouble to take a few pills, a powder, a glass of meat extract, or a draught of elixir, than to exert one's body, even if only for a quarter of an hour. Yes! and it is more refined, more aesthetic, it sounds more aristocratic , to go through a hydropathic cure, than to devote one's attention to these " brutalising " physical exercises.

But how I pity such people !

The curing of disease is the doctor's business, but practical experience teaches that they generally regard its prevention as beyond their sphere. So we must look after that ourselves. We do not arrange matters here as they do in China, where doctors are paid to keep people well. And what is required of us to ensure health is in reality so little, costing a mere trifle in comparison with apothecaries' drugs and patent medicines. The body, so patient under neglect that one often wonders at it, is just as grateful the moment a little attention is paid to it.

And when prompt and certain results can be guaranteed, and the thing may be done without special apparatus or preparations, is it not worth while to give it a trial ?

DIFFERENT SYSTEMS OF HOME GYMNAS- TICS

Thirty-five Years' Experience

Exercise of every organ and muscle, and a bath which is not to cost money or much time or trouble, can only be had within the four walls of the home. The blessings of home gymnastics are, therefore, accessible to each and every one who only cares to hold out his hands for them.

Let me tell a little about myself. My father suffered from different bodily infirmities, when I was born I only weighed 3 1/2 lbs, and could be placed in an ordinary cigar-box. When I was two I nearly died of dysentery; as I grew older I contracted every childish complaint, and in my early school-days I was always ill some few times in the year (with fever-ish colds, diarrhæa, etc.). I consequently neither inherited my present health and strength, nor laid the foundations of it in my childhood.

They are qualities acquired through physical exercises, which have been carried out on a plan which has been, year by year, more carefully thought out. Of course I should have attained this good result much more quickly and easily had I set about the matter at first with the knowledge and experience I now possess. But for that reason I regard it as my duty to render the work easier for those who are striving towards the same goal, but have not yet attained it.

In 1874, when I was eight years old, I got hold of some books translated from the English and German on " The Principal Teachings of Physiology " (Dr. A. Combe), and on " Health Gymnastics " (Dr. Schreber), and I began to do a few exercises on my own account both with and without-dumb-bells. A short notice on"Pedestrianism" in "Ueber Land und Meer " in 1880 taught me amongst other things to run on the balls of the feet, and was the first step towards my being able later—after having studied Victor Silberer in 1885—to introduce walking and running sports on rational lines into Denmark. In 1881 I studied a short popular " Guide to the Care of the Health " by Trautner, district Medical Officer of Health. Many learned men of today would do well to make themselves acquainted with its contents, and put them into practice.

I tried, one after the other, every system of Home Gymnastics that came out, and in addition, as years went by, gained considerable experience by practising Gymnastics (partly private and partly club practice), now according to the " Danish " method and now according to the " Swedish," as well as all kinds of out-of-door sports. Still, it was chiefly my private home gymnastics and running in the open air that transformed me from a delicate boy into a strong young man.

My first free and dumb-bell exercises were anything but systematic. Later on I tried various real systems requiring to be performed with weights hanging from a cord worked by a pulley. These apparatuses were comparatively difficult to set up, noisy to use, and quickly got out of order. Excellent exercises for the development of the muscles could be performed with their help, but no heed was paid to the well-being of the equally important internal organs, apart from the fact that it generally took quite an hour to go through all the exercises. The same objections hold against many English, American, and German sets of apparatus and the systems appertaining thereto, the principle of which is similar, though the resistance produced by stretching an elastic band is substituted for the weights. These band show ever soon grow slack and are easily broken, so that the necessary apparatus is dear in the long run.

Sandow's system with light dumb-bells has been very widely propagated, and is known half over the globe. It is an adaptation of the system of his master, Professor Attila. I myself made use of it for several years, though in a somewhat modified form. Of the 18 exercises of the system the first 13 are arm exercises demanding great exertion, which, of course, is not a happy arrangement. One is compelled to make many pauses in order to rest the arms, and the whole thing becomes too long drawn out, monotonous, and tedious. Mr. W. R. Pope, an ardent admirer of Sandow, in his " Physical Development " —in which he comments upon the system,— proposes that the time absorbed by these necessary pauses should be spent in posing in various attitudes! The system is a good one for producing strong arm muscles; but verily the body's vital force does not reside in the arms. I know not a few men who have very strong arms, but unwholesome blood, and delicate lungs and stomachs. It is of more importance to have vigorous lungs and heart, a healthy skin, powerful digestion, and sound kidneys and liver quite apart from the fact that it is unsightly for the arms to be proportionately more developed than the rest of the body. And the requirement which Sandow's system makes, namely, that, except during Exercise 13, the dumb-bells shall be tightly grasped the whole time, has for result that the thoughts, even during the few trunk and leg movements, are concentrated on the muscles of the arms. If one were to draw up a list of the different parts of the body in the order of the importance which is laid upon their development in Sandow's system, it would be as follows :

1. Muscles of the forearm.
2. Upper part of the arm, and shoulders.
3. Some of the muscles of the legs and trunk, and
4. The lungs and skin, which receive hardly any direct attention. Finally, the question of a good carriage is altogether neglected in Sandow's system. Most of the figures in his books and tables are consequently round-backed and knock-kneed. Ling's Swedish System often goes to the opposite extreme, in as much as it aims exclusively at producing an

exaggerated uprightness, at the expense of other equally important points. "My System" steers a middle course between these two extremes.

Sandow's own physical development is not ideal ; his limbs are too thick in proportion to their length and his somewhat small stature. He resembles the sluggish, clumsy figures of the Renaissance, which are far inferior to the types of antiquity in health, general strength, speed, and staying power, as well as in grace and elegance.

But one is compelled to admire the genius with which, though a German-born, professional athlete, he has managed to make a great part of the English-speaking world believe that he is the most perfect specimen of physical development in existence. And that he has used his authority in order to do a great deal of good, one is bound to concede.

Sandow, in his paper, "Sandow's Magazine for Physical Culture," Jan., 1904, page 55, says that my abdominal muscles are "almost abnormally developed," but I should like to make the following remarks : Compared with the recognised ideals of antiquity, all the athletes of the present day are very poorly developed round the waist. When the picture to which Sandow alludes was taken, I was far short of having my oblique abdominal muscles as fully developed as they are for instance in the Doryphoros of Polycletos, and for that matter, there is still something lacking : consequently, in spite of Sandow's criticism, I shall continue for some time yet to exercise those muscles in particular. I can allow an iron ball weighing half a cwt. to be dropped from a height of 4 feet on my naked abdomen, or a man weighing 216 lbs. avoirdupois and wearing thick-soled boots to jump 8 feet and land on the aforesaid part of my body, or an iron-tyred wheel-barrow with a load of 360 lbs. avoirdupois to be wheeled over me. The model of the above-mentioned statue, however, must have been capable of supporting the weight of a small locomotive on his abdomen —and his body has

18

been held up both by antique and modern artists and critics, as the normal, as a pattern and standard of perfection !! Moreover, it will be seen hereafter that my System is almost diametrically opposed to Sandow's.

The principal advocate of Physical Culture in America is Bernarr Macfadden, whose writings show talent and hygienic perception; Irving Hancock dedicated his book on "Japanese Physical Training" to him in the following words : "To one who has devoted the best years of his life to the betterment of American physique and health."

Finally, there is a little book by Dr. Gulick, an American : "Ten Minutes' Exercise for Busy Men." The idea is excellent, but the way in which it is carried out somewhat deficient. For one thing, six exercises offer too little variety in the time, especially as two of them are " stationary running."

There is doubtless no one who will refuse to admit that I thoroughly understand and am fond of running (the primary exercise of classic times), but as a part of indoor gymnastics, it should not be introduced in any form whatever. If the running be gentle, it loses its chief value as a gymnastic exercise ; if it be violent, the air of the room is set in motion, and the dust whirled up and absorbed during one's forced respiration. Besides which, there is no sense in using up any of the short and precious minutes of our Home Gymnastics in performing badly an exercise which one has an opportunity—for instance, on returning from one's daily work,—of performing well in the fresh air.

Before concluding this chapter I must likewise mention the numerous "inventors" of "secret" home gymnastic systems who have sprung up of late years. These are not accessible to the public in cheap books, but, by the aid of puffing advertisements, people are induced to pay exorbitant prices for information as to the exercises. As the latter are drawn up on old familiar principles, they are generally of some benefit, and of course there are always people who are attracted by the mysterious, and who imagine that so long as a thing is thoroughly expensive, it must necessarily be excellent as well.

What I understand by Exercise, Athletic Sports, and Physical Culture.

By Exercise I understand every kind of bodily exercise. By Athletic Sports I understand movements and exercises which are performed for pleasure or amusement, in order to enable one to excel others in any special branch, or to win in competitions. By Physical Culture I understand work performed with the conscious intention of perfecting the body, mind, and soul, and increasing one's individual health, strength, speed, staying power, agility, suppleness, courage, self-command, presence of mind, and sociable disposition. Strictly speaking, one and the same exercise can, subjectively regarded, be sport at one time and gymnastics, or physical culture, at another. A man who sits in a boat and rows, to strengthen his lungs and the muscles of his back, is performing a physical culture exercise, whereas it is, more often than not, sport for a so-called gymnast to vault the horse as high as he can manage, or even for him to strive to make the descent in a high jump as faultlessly as possible. Further, when a teacher of gymnastics tries to get his team to perform free exercises as nearly together as possible, so that they may be able to do better than other teams with which they are to be matched, even when there is no prize nor public mention in prospect, that is often only sport too. If, after a completed course of physical exercises, the question asked be: "What can the pupils do?" the thing is sport, but if it be: "How are they now physically ?" then it is Physical Culture.

The moment bodily exercises are chosen in such wise that they tend to the improvement and development of the individual in just those particular points in which he is deficient, they are rational Physical Culture. It ensues from this that a system of gymnastics, wrongly applied, may prove in the highest degree irrational for the individual, even if ever so rational in theoretical form. For anæmic boys or girls, rubbing, sun baths, and swimming will be a more rational form of Physical Culture, than exercises in a drill-hall, even according to Father Ling's system.

Physical Culture exercises can only be rational in their application when they take into consideration the needs of the individual. For that reason, team exercises and school-drill can never be more than approximately rational, and, carried on as they are in most cases nowadays, they are anything but that.

If the above-mentioned rower's comparatively weakest points were his lungs and back, his rowing might very well be rational Physical Culture. When a man, in a " Weight-lifting " Club, holds up an iron ball in the air for the sake of beating the existing record, that is Sport ; if he do so for the sake of developing his extensors, it is Physical Culture, and if it be his arms, and in particular the triceps which are comparatively weak, it is conceivable that he is performing rational Physical-Culture exercises. Still, I have never seen any man or woman whose arms were weak in comparison with their skin, or abdominal muscles.

For 35 years I have used my eyes and thought about these things, and I have come to the conclusion that those parts of the human body which in the majority of cases are farthest removed from ideal health and perfection of form are the skin and the middle of the trunk, for which reason skin gymnastics and exercise of the muscles about the waist are what nine people out of every ten stand most in need of. A system of gymnastics paying requisite attention to these points will have a good chance of being rational, especially in its practical application as Health Culture in the Home.

My System.

A quarter of an hour daily is a very limited time, but when it is used to the best advantage it is, nevertheless, sufficient to prevent illness and preserve health, indeed in many cases regain it, so that the body is little by little transformed from a fidgety, hypochondriacal master to an efficient and obedient servant. If you will concentrate your attention for 15 minutes on working for your health, you will get so far that in the remaining 1,425 minutes of the day you need not think of it at all. It is the very people who assert that corporal matters ought not to occupy one's thoughts, whom one always hears talking about their nerves, bad digestion, tiredness, and every imaginable kind of physical disability.

Only read one of the many patent medicine advertisements, that of Pink Pills for instance, and you will see drawn up a choice of the ills lying in wait for those who will not take a little rational exercise every day,—of course I do not mean that they ought to take the pills !

In all previous systems, the care of the skin is only, as it were, a step-child. Nevertheless I maintain that if a person can only spare a quarter of an hour a day for the practical care of the body, a bath, with subsequent rubbing, and airbath, is the most essential thing, whether there be facilities for a proper waterbath, or only for a damping of the whole body with a wet towel. As, however, in a quarter of an hour there is time for considerably more than a bath, I have drawn up, as well, a selection of the most useful and appropriate exercises, certain of which have been borrowed from well-known gymnastic systems, but the greater part thought out and put together by myself. I tried every way before the eventually placing the bath in the middle of the exercises: only practical order which renders it possible for ordinary people to take both water and air bath and perform the exercises with open windows, in the winter, without getting cold. Formerly I used to spring straight out of bed and take my bath first, but by so doing one easily becomes chilled before one has finished drying oneself, "bed-warmth " not lasting so long as the real warmth which comes of a series of exercises. There is another objection to taking the bath first, viz. : that you get into a perspiration and feel the want of another bath if you go through the exercises dressed ; and if one drills without clothes, some of the exercises cannot be performed without one either growing cold or (in the case of those done lying down) becoming dusty again. And if you wait to take your bath last, you undo the effect of the health-giving skin gymnastics, it being too cold to take a waterbath after an airbath.

Even people of the so-called educated classes may be heard to exclaim : "What need to take a bath every day ? One cannot possibly get one's body so dirty, if one change one's linen frequently, and do no dirty work !"

In the first place, I would reply : The loose dirt which comes from without is perhaps blacker, but is not so dangerous as the dirt, consisting of waste matter and poisonous substances, which is given off through the skin in much larger quantities than most people think, and which can be partially absorbed again to poison the body, if it be not removed every day. As a proof of the facility with which substances from without can penetrate through the skin to the internal organs, let me mention that if a solution of salicylic acid be rubbed into the skin, salicylic acid can be detected in the urine a few hours later.

And it is not only very injurious to oneself, but very objectionable to those others whose sense of smell has not been blunted by an unhealthy mode of life, to allow perspiration and grease from the skin to stay and putrefy, and be partially reabsorbed by the body. As a rule people are shy of saying such things to one another, but I do not intend to beat about the bush. It is well that people who do not take baths should be told that, even if there be no outwardly visible signs, the fact is patent to one's sense of smell. When such a person has been in our office or my room for one minute—and the windows are always open—I am obliged to have the door open as well, for a time, that the draught may blow the pestilential vapours away. I am not by any means talking of the products of respiration, or intestinal gases, but purely and simply of ill-smelling emanations from the skin. And this does not refer only to people of the "working" classes. I have often met "gentlemen" in frock-coats and top-hats and ladies in evening dress of whom you could tell by the smell of them, even at a distance of several feet, that they seldom or never took a bath. It is a special smell, just as people who are addicted to alcohol, for instance, have their peculiar smell. Supposing the person in question to have bad breath and perhaps be short-sighted as well, so that conversation is regarded as impossible unless the distance between one's face and his be reduced to a few inches, we have an exceedingly disagreeable but uncommonly frequent situation.

In the next place, the bath and the rubbing are intended to serve as skin gymnastics, acting upon the capillary vessels and nerves of the skin, and rendering them sound, healthy, and hardy—which is of the greatest possible importance to the body's general health. One can lay it down as a rule that the good or illtreatment of the skin has an immediate effect on the whole general state of one's health. The skin is not a sort of impermeable covering of the body, but is in itself one of its most important organs ; we feel with, and partially breathe through it, and we use it to regulate the warmth of our bodies, and to pass off obnoxious matter. It is very beneficial, indeed almost necessary for the health, to perspire a little every day, so long, be it observed, as one washes immediately after. But if there be no immediate opportunity for this, it is essential to keep in movement so as to maintain perspiration until home or some bathing establishment can be reached. How many thousands have contracted consumption, or the germs of other diseases, through transgression of this rule! This is especially the case with soldiers, who frequently, after sweat-inducing field exercises and other kinds of exertion, are compelled to remain absolutely inactive for a long time in the cold and wind, or if it be summer in the shade. A great deal of harm could be avoided in such cases if a dry towel, which could be carried in the knapsack, were passed over the breast and back, even if this were done under the shirt only. It always seems to me to be almost suicidal for a lady heated after dancing, or a perspiring cyclist, to sit down and eat an ice, or to drink cold beer. To grow cold while " wet " is always dangerous, whether the moisture be caused by perspiration, rain, or by falling into water with one's clothes on. During evaporation a very large amount of warmth is drawn from the body, and this has the worse effect for the very reason, especially when the moisture proceeds from perspiration, that the process of cooling is very unequal.

To be "dry-cold," on the other hand, is not so dangerous; yet it is exactly this of which people have such a horror, and this is why they pack themselves into so many clothes that they break out into perspiration with every little movement, the consequence being that they catch cold at once. People take cold very frequently, not because they are insufficiently clad, but because they wear too many and too thick articles of apparel. It is far less dangerous to take sun-baths in the open air during the cold season of the year; yet this again is regarded as terribly imprudent, so perverse is the public mind regarding such matters.

I have often heard people, even sportsmen and athletes, boast that they could do this, that, and the other without getting into a perspiration some indeed were so " strong " that they could not perspire at all. They were proud of what was very much to their disgrace. The pores of their skin were choked with clotted grease and dirt until they could not perspire, while their muddy complexions or flabby appearance were infallible signs of their unwholesome condition.

If the functions of the skin are wholly interrupted, death will ensue in the course of a few hours. Who does not know the story of the little child who was to represent the Golden Age in a procession at the accession of Pope Leo X., and had its whole body gilded over ? A few hours after-wards it breathed its last in convulsions.

The three chief aims of my System are to promote :

    1. The functions of the skin,
    2. The action of the lungs, and
    3. The digestion.

It will be seen that I give the place of honour in my system to the care of the skin. First come 8 exercises, the gradually increasing difficulty of which is calculated to induce a perspiration to break out at the end : next, the bath with subsequent thorough drying of the body : and after that 10 composite rubbing exercises, to be performed in air-bath costume, during which the surface of the entire body gets thoroughly and systematically polished. The rubbing is done with the palms of the hands, and should be a simple stroking or friction to begin with ; later on, as one's strength increases, it should be so vigorous that it becomes a sort of massage, if not for the internal muscles further from the surface, at any rate for the thousands of small muscles connected with the vessels of the skin, which are strengthened and developed more in this manner than by any other mode of procedure whatever.

After you have followed up my System for some time, the skin will assume quite a different character; it will become firm and elastic, yet smooth and soft as velvet and free from pimples, blotches, spots, or other disfigurements. Many have recommended of late a revival of the custom of the ancient

Greeks, viz. : that of performing physical exercises without clothing. Still one requires to be very much hardened—ordinary people could not possibly stand it at first—to do ordinary gymnastics in front of an open window during the cold seasons of the year. My rubbing exercises, on the contrary, can be carried out under such conditions, even by those most susceptible to cold. As a matter of fact, one keeps warmer, whilst doing them perfectly nude, than when standing still with all one's clothes on. As a proof of this I may state that I can easily keep comfortably warm in the open air, even when it is freezing, or a cold wind is blowing, whilst I am going through my rubbing exercises, whereas I might sit and shiver driving in a carriage in the same weather with all my clothes and an overcoat on. This may sound strange, but it is nevertheless true. I can only say, " Try it yourself." The secret lies in the fact that a solid warm this produced on the surface of the skin where it has been rubbed, even if only lightly, and this warmth lasts several minutes ; nor does it disappear whilst other parts of the body are being rubbed in their turn, so long as one proceeds according to a settled plan. The parts that might suffer most from cold receive in " My System " the most rubbing.

The next most important requirement of such a system is that it should develop and strengthen the lungs, the respiratory muscles, and the heart, and thereby promote the circulation of the blood and the waste and reconstruction of the tissues of the body. For this reason, after twelve of the exercises, a pause of 12 seconds has been allowed for two very deep, or three fairly deep, easy respirations. After Exercises Nos. 10, 13, and 14, pauses of only half that length are allowed, and after No. 9 none at all is necessary ; again, there is a threefold pause just before the bath, that there may be time for 3 or 4 respirations, getting the bath ready and stripping off the few clothes one has on. It is very right and proper to be in a perspiration before the bath, but the respiration and especially the pulsation of the heart should have become normal again. With regard to the heart, it is of the very greatest importance that these particular breathing exercises be never omitted ; while not for one moment must the breath be held during the performance of the 18 exercises proper, but it must be inhaled and exhaled deeply, quietly, and uninterruptedly through the nose all the time. It is absolutely necessary that the air one breathes should be good. Consequently, if the exercises are to be performed in the morning immediately on springing out of bed, the latter should be covered up again as quickly as possible (of course to be properly aired later on), and then the exercises may be done in the bedroom itself, provided the windows have been open all night. If not, they must be performed in an adjoining room, the window and the door of which have been open during the night. I can, however, hardly believe that anyone who takes the least interest in his or her health would sleep without giving free circulation to the fresh air through open Windows. My three little boys are bigger and healthier than any other children of the same age that I have seen. The eldest only slept with closed windows the first 10 days of his life (in a private Maternity Hospital) ; and the two younger have never, either summer or winter, been in a room with closed windows since the night they were born. Nevertheless, they have never had a trace of cold or cough. I only mention this to reassure those who are afraid of "the night air." I myself have slept with open windows since I was eight years old.

If afraid of not being warm enough at night, during the winter, it is very much better to put more clothes on the bed, or warmer night-garments on, than to close the window. The air you inhale can, and should, be cool and fresh.

I have ranked a good digestion as the third of the main pillars of health. The exercises which promote this have at the same time an excellent effect on the kidneys and liver. By giving these internal organs natural massage, and squeezing them, much as one squeezes a sponge, they will be strengthened and cease to give rise to the hundred and one different complaints to which people leading sedentary lives are subject. No less than than 11 of the exercises in "My System" act directly on the internal organs and vigorously stimulate the muscles enclosing them which are hardly ever called into use by every-day occupations. These are Nos. 1, 3, 4, 6, 7, 11, 12, 13, 16, 17, and 18. The same applies in a lesser degree to Exercises 2, 8, 14, and 15. After a few weeks' work you will note with agreeable surprise that the fat round your waist and abdomen is beginning to yield place to firm muscles, and indeed what I might call a "muscular corset" is gradually developed : the basis of a strong and healthy body. In women, moreover, this corset will bring about the conditions necessary for painless delivery in childbirth, together with other desirable results. What these "Corset exercises" also to a very high degree tend to promote in those who practise them are : a good carriage, a straight, erect back, and elasticity and suppleness in all the movements of the trunk.

It will be seen that I have, so to speak, only one special arm exercise (No. 8), and I was doubtful about including even this one, since in reality the arms, as also the muscles of the hand and breast, are strengthened by all the rubbing exercises. But as these, in common with one's every-day work, chiefly call the flexor muscles into use, whereas No. 8 is an exercise for the extensors, I have retained it, partly for that reason, and also partly because it simultaneously stretches nearly every muscle of the body and is therefore adapted to bring one into a perspiration just before the bath. Exercises apparently for the arms, such as Nos. 5 and 13, are quite as much for the muscles of the shoulders, the breast, the abdomen, the sides, the hips, and the back.

The beautiful and very important thoracic muscles, to which surprisingly little attention has been paid in all previous books on gymnastics, are developed in as many as 12 of my exercises.

Neither are there many distinct leg-exercises in my System. In the first place, exceedingly strong legs are not an essential to health ; in the next place, the best leg-exercises [running, quick walking, and jumping] cannot conveniently be carried out within doors, and in the third place most persons' legs, especially in towns, are well developed in proportion to the rest of their body (as one has ample opportunity of observing on a sultry summers day, when people come in crowds to take their " dip " in the sea). There are plenty of people who go for a walk every day, or go backwards and forwards between their home and their business, on foot, but very few of them take any other physical exercise. A little more attention, however, has been paid to those leg-muscles which, in an ordinary way, are seldom exercised,—thus the abductors and adductors are strengthened by Nos. 6 and 14, the tibialis anticus by No. 3, and the lower muscles of the calf by heel-raising. Exercises which are apparently for the legs, like Nos. 12 and 15, are intended, first and foremost, to act upon the internal organs, and in the next place to render possible rubbing in the manner pointed out. The Exercises Nos. 16, 17, and 18 are a great strain on the muscles of the trunk, if these are unpractised, and should therefore at first be performed quite slowly.

Some of the exercises (Nos. 1, 3, 4, 5, and 7), it might be thought, would be more effective if performed with dumb-bells, but this is so far from being the case, that even the strongest athlete will find he gets quite sufficiently vigorous exercise by going through the System without them. I myself left off using them altogether after gradually noticing that the exercises performed briskly and with precision produced at least as beneficial a result without dumb-bells as when I had fairly heavy weights in my hands.

Besides which, most of the exercises are either "resistance" or "arresting" exercises, in which one can oneself exert all the strength one has at command, either by pressing against the object selected (in the case of the rubbing exercises, the body), or by arresting the movements of the limbs and changing the direction of those movements. A child, a slight woman, or an old man, on the other hand, can perform the exercises in the easy degrees without over-exertion.

Before dismissing the question of the selection of the exercises themselves, I would emphasise further, that from amongst muscular exercises equally good in other respects I have chosen those which thoroughly exercise the joints, suppleness and mobility in every joint being the primary condition essential to carrying one's youthful buoyancy with one into old age.

Another thing required of a Home Gymnastic System that shall be attractive and accessible to all, is that it should also be cheap and easily intelligible. If I take a great many pages to explain the exercises, this is not because they are difficult to learn,—anyone who has done gymnastics at school will understand them at once—but because I wish to give absolutely exact and detailed instructions, so that I may be sure no one will go about them the wrong way. I have often seen Sandow's exercises, for instance, carried out incorrectly, even by teachers, because the explanations of the system were insufficient.

As " My System," in the next place, does not require any special apparatus whatsoever, there is no question of other expense than that of a so-called " sponge-bath." The cheapest costs about 10s. 6d., and is indestructible. On account of its flat shape, a bath of this sort takes up very little room, if, after use, it be placed against the wall or under the bed. Should you wish to be very lavishly provided, you can also buy a hand shower-bath for a few shillings. It is possible to avoid all expense, however, by using an ordinary tub, or by simply standing on a mat and slapping the body smartly all over with a towel dipped in cold or lukewarm water, or, in the event of no towel being handy, by wetting the body with the hand. Large sponges are expensive, and soon become greasy and nasty.

In the case of beginners the rate at which each exercise is performed depends primarily upon the rate of the breathing, and may be found to occupy 25 to 30 minutes, on account of the necessary references to the text or illustrations. When one is thoroughly practised in the System, however, the whole series can easily be performed in 15 minutes, as is shown in the time-table on pages 94 and 95.—The first few days the whole body will feel tender, but that need not trouble one, it is only muscular "next day" or "growing pains," which wear off if one keeps on. I have always felt satisfaction in these little pains myself, because they made me realise that the muscles that pained me were growing stronger. Still anyone who finds the pain too severe can rest a few days, and take self-massage, or rub himself with spirit, embrocation, or the like.—It is a matter of indifference whether one goes through the System in the morning, in the middle of the day (when changing one's clothes), or in the evening before going to bed ; but not unless some few hours have elapsed since the last meal. Should it be found that exercise just before bedtime causes disturbed slumbers, a different time should be selected at first. Or, last thing before getting into bed, after the exercises, stand still and rise 50 or 100 times on the toes. Later on, when the nerves have grown steadier, you will only sleep the better for your evening exercise.—It is an excellent plan, for those who have time, to go through the whole System, with the bath, in the morning, and then repeat the rubbing exercises by themselves in the evening. It should be remembered, however, when the rubbing exercises are taken by themselves, always to begin with Exercise No. 11, or, still better, to transpose No. 9 and No. 11. These ten rubbing exercises, with breathing-pauses, take but a bare 5 1/2 minutes to go through, yet have for result that you lie down in bed with a delightful feeling all over the skin, and fairly certain of a good night's rest. No one ought to deny himself these 5 1/2 minutes.

If you take a cold, or lukewarm, bath every day, you need never waste time or money in warm baths, whether Turkish baths, or any other kinds of expensive baths that are more or less humbug. But on the other hand, once a week, say on a Saturday, you should wash in your own bath with warm water (95° Fahrenheit) and soap, " sluicing " yourself well all over afterwards with a jug or hand-douche full of colder water.

A very practical mode of procedure—just as effective, but considerably cheaper than a Russian or Finnish bath,—is to run or walk quickly home from work, so as to get into a heavy perspiration, then take a bath at once, and go through the rubbing exercises, before dressing again for your midday or evening meal. You must, of course, put other clothes on, at any rate other underclothing. Let me, at the same time, call attention to the fact that it is an unhealthy and uncomfortable habit to wear the same underclothing night and day ; what is worn during the night ought to hang up to air during the day-time. When hardened you might find it pleasanter to lie quite unclothed in bed, at all events in the summer. For long enough I took no other exercise than the above-mentioned run home, with a bath and rubbing exercises afterwards, and yet kept in splendid condition. And no one can say that it cost either time or money, as I got home more quickly than by tram, and saved a penny.

No one ought to take a cold bath unless comfortably warm. The more one is perspiring, the colder one can bear the bath, and the more enjoyable it vvill be. But if one be feeling cold, and for any reason cannot get up the circulation, the bath should be warm.

When, during the summer, it is possible to bathe out of doors, the exercises can be performed at the bathing place, where one will generally be able to arrange matters in such a way that they can all be performed in their proper order. After a fairly long swim, if cold, the rubbing exercises will be the best means of restoring the circulation. It is a very good plan to undress at once; in the sunshine especially you do not want to keep your clothes on for the exercises preceding the bath. People who cannot stand a bright sun on their heads should wear a straw hat or a white handkerchief as a protection. As a general thing, you should let the sun shine on your body (not forgetting the back) whenever you have the chance. By so doing you lay up a store of health for yourself that you can draw upon in the gloomy season of the year. The ancient Greeks well knew how to appreciate sunshine as a health-giver, and, indeed, looked with contempt on a man with a white, spongy skin. Later on, like so much other valuable knowledge, this sank into oblivion, until rediscovered by Arnold Rikli, and Professor Finsen.

But there are still only comparatively few who properly appreciate the health-giving properties of the sun's rays. Even in hospitals, where people go to be made well, the blinds are drawn down to keep out the sun even in the winter months, when it shows itself so sparingly, and is so badly wanted ; but those who treat it with contempt do not escape unpunished ! After all, it is ridiculous to talk of any embarrassing warmth from the sun in Northern European climates. I will compromise as far as to except the really warmest summer months. But all the rest of the year, we ought rather to bring about the lesser degree of warmth we desire by opening more doors and windows, than by calling blinds, curtains, and awnings into requisition. The loss that may possibly be entailed in private dwellings by damage to the furniture coverings, and so forth, will be more than compensated for by improved health and increased capacity for work. As it is the rays of light, and not the heat of the sun, which have such a beneficial effect on the skin, and through it on the health of the whole body, we can derive great advantage in the summer, even very early in the morning, from a sun-bath of half an hour, which most people can manage to secure by getting up a little earlier. To make up for this we ought to provide for somewhat more sleep during the dark season of the year. We shall only be adapting our habits to little to Nature's own teaching. Babies, too, derive an extraordinary amount of benefit from crawling about, or playing, without clothes on, in the sunshine, or in warm weather. On the other hand it is a quite mistaken method of " hardening" children to let them go bare-legged during the cold seasons. It tends, rather, to hinder the growth of the legs. Head-coverings, however, are superfluous for children in almost all weathers, and grown-up people, too, ought to accustom themselves to going about bare-headed. This is the best way of avoiding baldness and nervous headaches, and one comes by degrees to regard the much-dreaded "draught" as a morbid superstition.

If obliged to practise the exercises indoors in the summer as well, you will probably be in a perspiration again before finishing the rubbing exercises. It will then only be necessary to wipe off the perspiration before dressing, with the half-wet towel which was used after the bath. This will make you feel comfortably cool. Or lie down for a few minutes under some light covering, especially protecting those parts sensitive to cold, until you feel that all surplus warmth has disappeared, but not longer; there must be no sensation of cold or of shivering. In exceptionally warm summer weather, all the exercises can be performed without clothing (with only sandals, or bedroom slippers, on), and in the following order: Nos. 11, 10, 1, 12, 2, 13, 3, 14, 4, 5, 16, 6, 17, 7, 18, 8, bath, drying of the body, Nos. 9 and 15. After each exercise the breathing-pause apportioned to it in the time-table should be taken (a 12 seconds' pause after No. 18). For very advanced students I can recommend the following order for the spring and autumn: bath, drying of body, Nos. 9, 15, put on sandals, 10, 1, 11, 2, 12, 3 (sitting upon a stool or chair), 13, 4, 14, 5, 6 (upon a lounge), 16, 7, 17, 8, and 18.

The Immediate Effects of Rational Physical Exercise.

The entire body is strengthened, and grows flexible, mobile, and efficient. After you have once really become strong all over, as a matter of course you are healthy as well, and if healthy, at the same time—but only then—really beautiful. This is true of both men and women. Beauty is thus identical with health and strength,—not a sign, but an expression of it. It can be proved, both amongst human beings and the higher animals, that the shapes and proportions which render the body most serviceable in every possible respect are the most beautiful and the most harmonious. I am not alluding to beauty of feature, or unnecessary strength of arm. Of what use can it be for a chain to have certain tremendously strong links, if others are fragile ? One must admit that it is an altogether erroneous mode of speech to call a man strong, just because the muscles of his arms are unusually powerful, while perhaps the sources of his vitality,—the muscles round his body, and his internal organs,—are weak. It may in fact be positively dangerous to the health to be much stronger in some of the limbs than in others, or than in the rest of the body. It induces one to overestimate one's capacities. Strains through lifting, stitch, rupture, and nearly every over-exertion of such organs as the heart, arise from this cause. It is as though, trusting to the strong links in the chain, one were to hang upon it as much as it would be able to bear, were the entire chain of the same quality.

The result naturally is that one of the weaker links gives way, and then the entire chain is broken. Not only have the strong links been of no use, but they have done a great deal of harm by creating a false impression.

But the idea of " strength " has been so much misunderstood, and the word so much misused, that people do not care to do anything in order to become really strong. They have seen again and again so-called strong men hampered by every kind of illness, and often dying at a comparatively early age. And the same with beauty. The erroneous conception that this depends on the contour of the face, the colour of the eyes, the luxuriance of the hair,—things which it is not easy to permanently alter, has resulted in people overlooking the beauty that is bona fide and valuable, and which, more over, it is in everyone's power to secure for himself. And yet a fresh complexion, clear eyes, and a free carriage of the head—all of which are the outcome of a rational care of the body—lend a certain beauty to the most irregular features. By following out my System, and now and again going for a run (on the balls of the feet), you will not only attain perfect health, but the shape and appearance of your body will approach more nearly every day to the ancient classical ideal of beauty, for the simple reason that this coincides exactly with the highest ideal of bodily health, flexibility, and all-round efficiency. And running is not for boys and men only; women, and especially young girls, ought certainly also to practise running long stretches in sportsmanlike style. Then by degrees we shall be spared the sight of a walking sylph, who absolutely must catch her tram, suddenly transforming herself into a cow or waddling duck.

The art critics of our day, in their remarks anent the classical statues of olden times, have certainly confused cause and effect, probably because they themselves are rather students than practical athletes, and therefore lack the qualifications necessary to understand what colossal and yet delicately and harmoniously balanced physical powers and what a mighty exuberance of strength are represented by a Doryphoros or an Apoxyomenos, and what a tremendous and unswerving labour must needs have preceded such a result. To imagine that it was love of beauty that produced such shapes and lines is simply absurd. The large, capacious chest so characteristic of all antique statues is synonymous with the highest possible degree of strength and endurance in lungs and heart. The powerful oblique muscles of the abdomen, which form the most beautiful part of the celebrated antique torso—a glaring contrast to the thin, unmuscular waists of our present-day athletes—are developed by the very exercises that I have cited above as most strengthening to the digestion and the intestinal functions. There are other muscles, as for instance the triceps (on the outside of the upper arm) and the trapezius (at the back and sides of the neck), which are often exaggeratedly developed in present-day athletes, whereas they are never strikingly conspicuous among the ancients.

They play no considerable role as regards the health or general efficiency of the body, which is the reason I have not laid much stress upon them in " My System."

The chief value and title to esteem of ancient classical sculpture is that it has created models we can admire, learn from, and seek to imitate.

Let me repeat what Dr. J. B. Hutchinson writes: "In ancient Hellas, Physical Exercise and Art stood in the closest relationship to one another. Without gymnastic exercises, Art would really not have existed at all. The ideals of human physical perfection for all future times were then created. Physical exercises ought to be taken very seriously, in view of their extraordinary influence on the preservation of the strength of the race. Everyone ought to feel it his or her duty to do the utmost possible to perfect the health, strength, efficiency, and beauty of their bodies. Parents ought to study their own constitutions and family history in order to counteract in their children possible hereditary defects or tendencies to delicacy. Everyone ought to strive to attain so great a measure of vitality and self-control, of physical, mental, and moral strength, that he or she may look to have children who are improved editions of their parents. Whoever intelligently brings up such children will have the honour of having rendered the greatest and noblest service to the state, namely, that of contributing to the raising of the level of our race as a whole.

"Pictures of the most beautiful statues of ancient and modern times, and especially of the former, ought to be hung up in every school, club, and gymnasium, and as far as is possible, life-sized casts should be set up as well, to accustom the eye to conceive the perfect form, to compel the beholder to value beauty of form, and to give the young ideals they can strive to imitate in their own bodies. At all sports and gymnastic celebrations, prizes ought to be awarded to those who can give proof of the best physical development. I have put this idea into practice on several occasions. The greatest honour for an athlete would not then be to possess cups and medals, but to be considered worthy of selection as model to a celebrated sculptor, and of being placed side by side with the statues of olden times. A new and noble held of activity would thus be thrown open, both to the ambition of the sportsman, and to the national art of the painter and sculptor."

THE MINOR SOURCES OF HEALTH

What I have hitherto recommended and included in "My System" in these pages, namely lung, skin, and muscular gymnastics in conjunction with fresh air, sunlight, and water, are the main sources of health. If one draws from them daily, one can afford to devote less attention to the minor sources. Although they have no place within the 15 minutes' limit, I will nevertheless briefly state my own experience with regard to them.

Suitable Diet.

There are more people who slowly eat themselves to death than there are who die of hunger. So do not always eat as much as you think you can stuff into you, especially at night. A great deal of the food will probably pass through undigested. This wears out your digestive organs before their time. You can see from this how foolish the wise man's words were when he said : " A man is what he eats." They ought rather to run : "What a man is, depends on how he eats," or "how he digests."

Leave off bolting your food; do not wash every mouthful down with a drink; and leave off reading the newspaper at meal-times, thus forgetting to masticate properly. Still you must not fancy that you can live to be 80 simply by chewing every mouthful 36 times. If you feel unwell, it will most often be because your stomach is overloaded, and in that case you will feel better for skipping a meal, or for fasting for a day and drinking nothing but water. The plainest meal will then taste delicious. Moreover, for the sake of the liver, our outpost against infection or poisoning, we ought not to eat too much or too rich food ; this particular organ thrives better on "trunk-circling" or " side-bending."

When your digestion has been invigorated through physical exercise you can safely eat almost every kind of food, but avoid vinegar, strong spices, and condiments, and remember that porridge and bread, potatoes and fruit, give one more strength and less gout than roast meat and beefsteak with onions. People who eat too much meat often suffer from tainted breath. How often have I not seen digesting of the so called " boatrace-steaks "exhaust a crew to such an extent that they came in far behind us others, who had only eaten a little bread or a plate of oatmeal porridge. I have seen big, strong Italians, whose fare consisted only of dry French rolls and thin coffee, work much harder and with greater endurance than for instance the Danish workmen, who are fed on meat and strong beer.

Richly prepared meat, highly seasoned dishes, things with vinegar (such as beetroot), sardines, lobsters, strong cheese, and so forth are poison to the stomachs of young people under sixteen. The same applies to such drinks as wine, strong beer, coffee, and tea. Even grown-up people would do well to remember that "strong drink makes weak men." But I am not a faddist. I believe in eating and drinking anything in moderation, because with a reasonable amount of good exercise the digestion is so enormously improved that one need not worry about what to eat and drink. A little spirits now and again on special occasions may not do much harm, but everyone who takes plenty of concentrated spirits daily ought to know that he is breaking down his health by so doing, and in any case his power of resisting disease.

Of the importance of a daily, regular evacuation of the bowels, I need not say much. I should first like to know whether anyone who goes through " My System " every day will be able to wait much more than 24 hours. Immediately after rising in the morning, just before going to bed at night, and perhaps also once in the course of the day, preferably mid-way between two meal-times, one or two glasses of fresh, clean water ought to be drunk. In this way, the intestines, and especially the kidneys, receive a wholesome bath. If the stomach needs cleansing, a little common salt may be added to the water.

Sensible Underclothing.

Ordinary coarse, loosely woven linen, which does not hinder evaporation from the skin, is a healthy and in the long run a cheap material both for shirts and drawers, but it should not fit closely. A pure linen mesh (or loose tricot) may be mentioned as the healthiest material for underclothing, but is somewhat more expensive. Woollen and flannel clothing is too warm, and shrinks in the wash, thus getting too tight and making the skin tender and irritable. A generation ago most boys and young men went about without overcoats and wool underclothing, according to the comparatively healthier practice of their fathers. Then thick, tight, woollen under-vests won their way into favour and contributed considerably to the present generation's susceptibility to cold. I, too, wore wool for a number of years, and tried Jaeger's normal clothing for a long time, but I gained nothing by it except that I made myself tender and nearly always had a cold or cough.

When some years later I flung my woollen under clothing aside, my appetite was for a long time twice as large. As a matter of fact, metabolism,—the waste and renewal of bodily tissue—is impeded by unduly warm clothing. As a matter of course, woollen underclothing ought not to be left off with-out some previous hardening of the system by means of the daily bath and rubbing. But if there still be fear of taking a chill,a beginning can be made by wearing the woollen vest over the shirt, or a vest of linen mesh—not the garment worn all night, be it understood—may be put on under the starched shirt. The same can be done when you feel the cold in very severe weather, or when travelling. But after having made use of my rubbing system for some time, you will find that you do not feel the cold so easily, and will yourself find woollen clothes uncomfortable. My wife used to wear the following 7 articles of underclothing in the winter : woollen vest, abdominal belt, chemise, drawers, corset, lined knickerbockers, and a Jaeger camisole. Now, even in the severest weather, she never wears anything but a heavy linen-mesh combination under her dress. Apart from the comfort and convenience—which cannot be estimated,— the cost of this underclothing is less than one-third of the other. Only for protracted, sweat-promoting physical exercise in cold weather is a heavy but loosely-woven woollen vest or sweater desirable. There is now among the doctors in many countries a movement on foot against wool underclothing, which for that matter was rejected long ago by Hippocrates and that ancient Master of Hygiene, Moses. The late Dy. J. L. Milton , Senior Surgeon at St. John's Hospital, London, wrote that he had been advocating linen under-wear for 15 years. He had persuaded people of over 80 years of age to leave off flannel and woollen vests, and had never, despite the damp climate, seen any of the dreaded bad results ensue.

Dr. C. P. Ambier Asheville, New York, said at a medical conference, that he had put seven-year-old children and octogenarians from wool into linen underclothing without the slightest inconvenience to them even during the coldest winter weather. In Russia and Siberia, as also in hottest Africa, linen is almost solely used for underclothing.

The healthiest and most comfortable thing for people working in the open air, such as bricklayers, and agricultural labourers, would be to wear no clothes at all at their work in summer-time save short knee-breeches, and to put on their coats only when they went home from their day's work.

If wrestlers in a circus can show themselves bare to the waist, there will surely be no one who would forbid workmen doing the same for their health's sake. It ought to be tried. In 50 years' time it will be universal anyhow; why wait ? Better far to make short work of it and at once abandon the thick, ugly, woollen vest, heavy with putrefied grease from the skin and saturated with stale, evil-smelling perspiration ! I have often in times gone by, when on long rowing excursions in the Sound, got the whole crew to take their rowing vests off. The wind might blow, and we might sweat, but it was only to our own comfort and advantage.

In addition, everything should be avoided that is in any way confining, such as tightly buttoned wrist-bands or neck-bands, tight collars, and garters. Even apparently loose elastic garters can injure the legs. It was the fashion once among the Copenhagen street boys, and perhaps in other countries than Denmark, to put a small, thin elastic ring round dogs' tails. The victims felt nothing at first, and their owners also failed to notice the narrowband. But by degrees the tail shrivelled up and fell off!

Moderate Indoor Temperature.

What are we coming to ? In times gone by, nobody thought of heating bedrooms or churches; now we shall soon behaving heating-apparatus in trams and cabs. — Anything over 60° F. is not only not beneficial, but in the long run injurious, in a sitting-room. The body becomes a hot-house plant with no power of resistance. It is easy to accustom oneself to a lower temperature. In our office it is never more than 53° to 55° F. in the winter; even the lady bookkeeper finds it comfortable. My youngest boy has never, even when he was born, been kept in a higher temperature than 57° in the firing seasons of the year ; if he were cold, of course I should have more fire kept up. As it is, it is often only 48° in the children's bedroom, but a baby's bath should be from 104° down to 89° the first year. By having open windows day and night in the whole of our flat, I have managed to counteract the unfortunate circumstance—which in other places helps to bring about the death of many young children—that the sitting-rooms look towards the North, out on to a high, thickly-wooded bank, which makes it so dark that we have to light up in the middle of the day. I do not mean of course that less fuel should be burnt, but that there should be a window open, at least a little way, the whole time. —

Warm air that is fresh is naturally better than cold that is bad, and there cannot be sufficient ventilation without warming a room somewhat. To keep in the heat by shutting the windows costs less in firewood, but more in medicine, which is dearer.

Proper Care of Teeth, Mouth, Throat, and Hair.

It does not do to demand impossibilities of busy men, such, for instance, as that the teeth should be brushed after every meal, but bits of meat and the like should preferably be removed with a wooden tooth-pick.

The following may be regarded as the minimum that can entitle one to be called cleanly and sensible. Brush the teeth and gums up and down, as well as across, and do not forget to brush them inside, at least once a day, and at night very much rather than in the morning, when one might be satisfied with rinsing the mouth out and gargling the throat a few times with water containing a teaspoonful of salt. Let some relative (or better a dentist) look carefully at your teeth a few times in the year, to see whether there is any decay. If so, the tooth should be stopped at once; it pays in the long run.

Do not allow children to eat every day sweets, chocolate, or cakes with sugar upon them, and never hot, or cold, but tepid food. It is not enough to taste it oneself to see whether food is cool enough not to burn ; remember that a civilised tongue and palate are, so to speak, copperplated.

The hair must be thoroughly combed and brushed every day, and exposed as often as possible to the invigorating action of sun, wind, and rain. All artificial hair tonics and restorers are injurious.

Some Attention to the Feet.

A badly-tended foot has something corpse-like about it. But the prevalent opinion is that so long as a sepulchre is well whited, the surrounding world's sense of sight and smell will not be offended by the corpse. As a rule one may assume that the more elegant the cut of the shoe, the uglier and the more deformed the foot itself will be, whether that of a lady or a gentleman. Many people who seldom wash their bodies or their feet would not venture to show themselves in the street without their coat being brushed and their foot-gear polished, and regard it as absolutely necessary to put on a clean collar every day. Indeed I positively believe that by many people, even in " intelligent " circles, it is looked upon as natural and likely for the feet to be dirty, whereas the hands, of course, must always be spotlessly clean. Otherwise I cannot explain the following instances of, let us say, naiveté. I once overheard a fragment of a conversation between two female school-teachers : "Just fancy, his hands were as black as—oh ! what shall I say ? —yes, as my feet " And last year, at the swimming competition at the Royal Docks in Copenhagen, I saw a " gentleman " who was going to take part in one of the races walking about among the company with a student's cap and swimming costume on, and deformed feet as black as coal !

Has the care of the feet anything to do with health ? it may be asked. Yes ! in the first place, feet that have not been hardened give rise to many kinds of chills and worse illnesses, because they soon get cold, and cannot stand being wet, and in the next place, tender feet, suffering from one or more of the defects unfortunately so well known, render an otherwise capable body almost entirely helpless.

The greatest and most important part of what the feet require, however, the daily bath provides. One ought in addition to pay attention to the nails, and remove hard skin after the weekly warm bath—or at any rate once a month. Otherwise ingrowing nails, inflammation, etc., will sooner or later make the guilty parties rue their neglect.

Besides which, if you do not give the toes the air and freedom of movement which they, like the rest of the body, require, you will gradually induce perspiring feet, one of the most distressing complaints, resulting from dirt, that exist. When you come home in the evening, you ought always to take off your shoes and stockings at once, and either go about with bare feet, or else simply with sandals (flat leather soles with a few straps),—this is a very cheaply purchased comfort. Without one needing to think about it, the toes will very soon get movement and gymnastics on their own account. while you sit writing or reading. Ugly, angular, hard, or raw toes soon grow round, soft, and nice, through the use of stockings with a division for each toe (like gloves). And when once the toes are in good condition, the most comfortable and convenient thing of all is to go about with " airsocks," that is to say, with bare feet inside boots roomy enough to allow of a stratum of air everywhere, and, in the winter, of a fibre sock as well. In this way the skin grows strong, and is always dry and warm. For the rest I only long

for it to become customary to walk about in sandals in public streets and places.

I am not going to trench further on the question of grown-
up people's foot-wear. They insist, after all, on reserving to
themselves the right of wearing shoes too small and too
tight, and this applies also to stockings. But I should like to
put in a word for the innocent little ones. The Chinese often
squeeze the feet of their children, to keep them short ; we
squeeze them in another direction. It is six of one and half a
dozen of the other! Wherever you go, you see babies lying
asleep in their cradles (when once the poor little things have
squalled themselves to sleep), with tight stockings and
ready-made laced boots on their feet. The least punishment
that their mothers ought to be condemned to would be to
sleep a night in bed with stockings and laced boots on. In
the case of 99 per cent. of mothers it is from motives of van-
ity that their children wear shoes as small and smart as can
be procured, and it would certainly be impossible to get any
mother to admit that they are too small, even had one an
opportunity of drawing the outline of the foot on paper, and
proving how much wider it is than the sole of the shoe.

A bad carriage, a clumsy, hesitating walk, distorted feet, and
numberless hours of pain are the penalty of wearing, while
growing, shoes that are too small.

Eight Hours' Sleep.

This is, on an average, the minimum necessary if you do not
wish to burn the candle at both ends. But one may very well
sleep seven hours in the summer, and nine in the winter.
First-rate physical work cannot be performed unless one has
slept well the night before, as I have often found from experience, and I doubt whether correspondingly good mental
work can, either, unless with the help of nerve-destroying
stimulants. As far as the bed itself is concerned, feather-beds

should be avoided, and the head should not be too high. One small pillow is sufficient.

Moderation in Smoking.

An old English clergyman, who had smoked as a young man, remarked : "On many a minister's tombstone the words 'Died in the Lord' are engraved, when the inscription ought rather to be 'Smoked himself to death.'

All the boys one sees with cigarettes in their mouths—and their number is unfortunately legion—are physical, moral, and intellectual suicides.

A pipe or a cigar after lunch and dinner will hardly hurt a grown-up person; still, one has a fuller use of one's senses, especially those of taste and smell, if one does not smoke. I have frequently experienced this when in times gone by I have left off smoking for several months while training. You can also better participate in other enjoyments if you give up tobacco; you are better able, for instance, to play with your children in your leisure time. If you restrict yourself to one or two cigars or pipes a day, they will taste all the better.

SPECIAL REMARKS ON THE APPLICATION OF "MY SYSTEM."

For Infants.

Some very valuable information and instruction concerning the upbringing of children is contained in "My System for Children," which is issued by the publishers of this book, and particulars of which will be found at the end of the volume.

For Old People.

Fat, like rheumatism and stiffness, can be kept at bay by rational physical exercise every day. Most people think that they are too old for gymnastics as soon as they are over 30. This is a lamentable error. Physical exercise is the only unfailing means whereby one can preserve one's youthful strength, activity, and buoyancy, both of body and mind. "Yes, but if you have not gone in for this nonsense since you were a boy, it cannot be any use to set about it when you are 50 and begin to feel old!" But that is just it, it can!

Although "My System" has been before the public only for a few years,I have, nevertheless, received hundreds of letters from both men and women, of ages ranging from 50 to 80 years, declaring that by the use of "My System" they have become as if rejuvenated, and the only complaint they have to make is that they had not become acquainted with the System before they grew so old.

For Literary and Scientific Men and Artists

The minds of such men work according to other laws, and in higher spheres, than those of the uninitiated, and they are consequently inclined to overlook the fact that their bodies are subject to quite ordinary natural laws. If the body is not looked after, it will eventually rebel against the mind and prevent it from attaining its high goal. Most of the great composers and many poets died in their thirties. How many treasures of sound and how many valuable literary productions the world has lost simply because they took no thought for the health of their bodies !

It is especially advantageous for singers to develop their abdominal muscles.

The Hygienic Sense is not one that is acquired in the study. Unfortunately it is only too often lacking in those quarters where it might be of most use, that is to say, among the Sanitary Authorities themselves. In many countries Physical

Culture is a subject of scientific interest, whereas in scientific circles in Denmark it is a terra incognita. And yet there is matter in it for no end of theses and even treatises, which would have, into the bargain, a chance of proving considerably more generally useful than "The Eye of the Cod" or "The Vegetation of Madeira," for example.

For Office Workers

"Surely you do not want to saddle us with still more work ; we sit and toil all day as it is and have barely time to eat!" To this objection I would reply: Listen! When towards evening you are feeling tired and stiff from stooping, it is not a great relief for a moment (take care though that the chief does not see!) to throw yourself back in your chair and stretch out your arms and legs? Yet it is a very considerable muscular exertion, you can positively hear your joints crack. The quarter of an hour's extra work, which I have the audacity to try and impose on you, is of a similar nature, and has a similar, but a thousand times greater, effect. The town office type is often a sad phenomenon. Prematurely bent, with shoulders and hips awry from his dislocating position on the office-stool, pale, with pimply face and pomatumed head, thin neck protruding from a collar that an ordinary man could use as a cuff, and swaggering dress in the latest fashion flapping round the sticks that take the place of arms and legs ! At a more advanced age the spectacle is still more pitiable; the fashion in dress can be followed no longer, because a family must be fed; the eyes are dull, and the general appearance is either still more sunken and shrivelled or else fat, flabby, and pallid, and enveloped in an odour of old paper, putrefied skin-grease, and bad breath . —But things need not be so !

There is no necessity for work to leave so unpleasant a mark on a man. I was in an office for 13 years myself. Only spend one poor little 15 minutes a day in the way I have advised, and life will have much real pleasure to offer to you too !

And then you must try to make your principal understand that if he requires you to sit and inhale bad air all day, from ignorance, or to save the expense of ventilation, it is his fault if you get ill, now that you yourself are doing all you can in your spare time to improve your health !

What applies to people in offices applies likewise to those engaged in literary or other writing work, or in sitting or standing employment indoors.

For those devoted to Athletic Sports.

Everyone who is acquainted with the newest and best methods of rowing, swimming, putting the shot, throwing the hammer, the disk, or the 56-lb. weight knows quite well that the greatest tests of strength in such exercises can only be successfully met by allowing the chief work to fall on the muscles of the legs and trunk, whereas the man who, by dint of practising with heavy iron weights, or through Sandow's system, has acquired abnormally thick and knotty arm muscles, ignominiously fails. I have myself been an adept in all these exercises, so can speak from experience.

Perhaps it is not so well known that it is also in the highest degree advantageous for runners, quick walkers, and jumpers to have strong muscles round the waist. By means of the "Corset Exercises" (the name under which I include all the exercises which develop the above-mentioned muscles), a man can keep himself in training throughout the winter, even if he have no opportunity of running in the open air. What generally makes a runner, or other devotee of foot-sports, who is not in good training, give up, is not so much want of breath, or tired legs, as those well-known uncomfortable sensations in the abdomen, the diaphragm, and the sides and loins, which are summed up in the word " stitch."

In January, 1904, in thick winter clothes and heavy boots, I ran 7.15 miles over very hilly country through snow and slush, in one hour, and although I had not run for three months, did not feel the least "stitch," simply because I had done my "Corset Exercises" every day. In my younger days, when I was much lighter, but did not do these exercises, I should have got the stitch, under similar circumstances, before I had done a quarter of the distance. I am now (1911) 45 years of age, but still always fit for running five miles at a fair speed, keeping myself in condition simply by doing "My System" every day.

In selecting the exercises, I have endeavoured to pick out those likely to constitute the best preparation for young people wishing to attain proficiency in the above-mentioned health-giving and recreative physical exercises. Every athlete will find that following up " My System" is the easiest way of keeping himself in condition through the winter and at the same time of developing the muscles he most stands in need of.

In connection herewith, I can show, as curiosities, letters in my possession from many elderly gymnasts and athletes in which the writers inform me that formerly, despite a zealous pursuit of sport, they always had to complain of indigestion, and that their digestions only became regular after they had practised "My System" for some time.

I must seriously warn athletes against taking too much exercise without sufficient rest, food, and sleep. That is likely to produce a state of affairs (so-called overtraining) which makes one fall an easy prey to illness, and is a poor advertisement for any kind of sport, even if one has beaten the record. The question is not so much one of accomplishing, while training, a considerable or protracted and difficult task every day, as of getting the body into such a condition that it is able, without ill effects, to perform the required work when the time comes (for instance, in a race or competition). These principles are often greatly sinned against, and there is much to be learnt in this respect from the Americans, who are the finest athletic sportsmen in the world, and who lay most stress on bringing the entire body into a condition of the highest possible degree of health and vitality.

Many sportsmen, also, upset their hearts because they take no care to breathe properly. At the Olympic Games of 1906, it appeared that nearly all the participants, excepting the Americans, suffered from enlargement, or other defects, of the heart. Those who carry out "My System" according to directions will acquire the good habit of inhaling and exhaling deeply, both during the exercises as well as immediately after them. The reason why I have been able to take part, for a whole generation, in many and various hard and often protracted contests, without inflicting the slightest injury upon my heart, is because I have always from childhood paid strict attention to correct respiration.

For Women to Remember.

If only half the time that is now spent in dressing, or in curling and other ruination of the hair, were devoted to a sensible care of the body, there would be fewer unhappy marriages and fewer unsatisfactory children. This Vale of Tears would become a Paradise. All women wish for beauty, harmonious proportions, and a good figure, but possibly not one in a hundred of them knows what these really consist of, and that the only means of acquiring them—and in the case of older women, keeping them —is a daily bath, rubbing of the skin, and all round bodily exercise, together with going about in the fresh air and sunshine.

The present generation of grown-up women is doubtless almost past praying for. But perhaps, ladies, for your daughters' sakes, it may interest you to know that in 20 years' time men will have advanced so far in knowledge and appreciation of Hygiene, that they will no longer rest content with compassionating the woman who has made havoc of herself by wearing a corset (even if she have not tight-laced), but they will dub it stupidity, slovenliness, and idleness on her part to go about in a corset and neglect her daily bath and gymnastics. It will be an exceedingly uncomfortable position for a newly-married woman to find herself in if her husband has to point out to her how low she stands in the scale of civilisation, as regards the care of her health and beauty, and, baldly stated, her cleanliness, beneath her outward finery. A woman who leaves off her corset is, however, in ill case if she do not get something else in its stead to keep her warm and hold her body upright and together. Warmth comes quickly enough when the skin is awakened out of its lethargy by the bath and rubbing exercises. Medical books state that muscles which will support the body gradually develop of themselves, if the corset be left off, but these muscles, it is true, make their appearance very slowly or not at all, unless one performs exercises, such as those I have indicated, which are specially calculated to produce them, and with the help of which one can acquire a "muscular corset" in a few months. The secret of the beautiful figures of the female statues of antiquity lies in the fact that they all possess a corset of this kind in lieu of the modern expensive, ugly, perishable, uncomfortable, and unhealthy substitute.

"But we really have not time"!

Yes! you have! The more you have to do, the better you will understand how to arrange your time so that there will be one quarter of an hour to spare. And when you have once properly begun, you will look forward eagerly every day to this quarter of an hour and especially to the extraordinarily agreeable sensation that the rubbing produces all over the body.

This plea of lack of time very seldom indeed holds good, when you come to inquire more closely into matters. Many mothers declare that they have no time to bath themselves and their children every day, to do gymnastics with them, brush their teeth, see that their bowels work properly, get them out in the fresh air in all weathers, etc., but the same mothers have plenty of time to devour one novel after another, to chat with others of the same way of thinking on the stairs or at the corners of the streets, to parade the town, or go to tea-shops.

For Cyclists.

The bicycle is a splendid means for getting from the town atmosphere out into the fresh country air, quickly and independently of trains, and for returning again when duty calls. And as a means of conveyance for tourists it is invaluable. In all other respects, however, its importance for the health is negative. I rode a high bicycle as earlv as 1883, and afterwards, for many years, a safety both in winter and summer. But it dawned upon me by degrees that as a daily means of getting about, the cycle was not only in many respects bad for the health, but it tricked me out of the good exercise that a quick walk to and from business provides. So I left off cycling and have not since regretted it.

Rational games and sports on foot give a classical contour to the legs, whereas cycling in the long run deforms them. A brisk walk — not to speak of really quick walking—in addition to those of the legs, brings many of the other muscles of the body into play, whereas cycling develops some few of the leg muscles only, the other parts of the body being fatigued and prejudiced by being kept either constantly on the strain or wholly inoperative. A man who gets no exercise but cycling cannot avoid sundry parts of his body being defective, and he then fails a victim to divers illnesses. It is therefore still more important for the cyclist than for the pedestrian to get exercise of the muscles round the body, and those of the chest, the back, and the shoulders, every day. I do not believe this can be procured in any easier or more effective manner than by following out " My System."

For Country People.

Dear dwellers in the country ! You are world-renowned for your skill in cultivating the soil, breeding cattle, and making butter. You have also the reputation of being shrewd and sensible, and of not caring to spend money on useless things. Then why will you swallow all the expensive medicine that the doctor often only recommends you because you would otherwise say that he does not know his business? Hear what some of the shrewdest doctors in the world have said. Sir Morell Mackenzie (the Emperor Frederick's doctor) said : " If there were not a single drop of medicine in the world, the death-rate would be lower !" and Dr. Titus (the Court Physician at Dresden) said : " Three-quarters of the human race are killed by medicine." Nearly all medicine is poison; the more one takes, the less it helps in the place required, while the whole of the rest of the body gets poisoned.

It is scandalous that there should be so much illness in the country, where every condition exists for leading a perfectly healthy life. principal reason is that you really have not the least notion of caring for your skin.

It is bad enough that you have such a horror of fresh air in your rooms, but this is counteracted in a great measure by the air being so much better than in the town, the moment that you poke your nose outside the door. And exercise you nearly all get enough of, even if it be only partial. Among the factory-workers and the poor in large towns illness can be excused, but not among you. You get poisoned and out of sorts because you neglect your skin. And instead of seeking health by washing, grooming, and hardening it everyday (which you do for your horses and cattle, and in places even for your pigs), you gorge yourselves with still more poison in the shape of medicine, and muffle yourselves up in still more unnecessary clothing. The result of course is that illness will seize hold of you still more readily next time. One of your greatest inflictions, so much discussed and written about just now, I mean Consumption, owes to this its extraordinary dissemination in the country. Dr. Dettweiler, the celebrated tuberculosis specialist, said : "The tuberculosis patient is as much skin-sick as lung-sick." Neglect of the skin destroys a man's power of resisting bacilli.

Dr. P. Niemeyer says : "Dread of fresh air is the chief cause of tuberculosis. He who combats this dread does as much for the prevention of the disease as he who fights the bacilli."

What hot-beds of disease the small, overcrowded, and practically unventilated village schoolrooms are ! The air is either supersaturated with the varied emanations arising from crowds of dirty children, often mingled with steam from wet clothes and greased boots, or else it is heavy with smoke and dust from the stove. If a sensible schoolmaster attempt to open the windows during a lesson, he gets all the parents down upon him.

The gymnastics pursued in many places with such ardour might be of benefit to the health of you country people; but, as things are, they tend to do more harm than good, by reason of your very deficient comprehension of the care of your skin and the need for fresh air. I have frequently witnessed voluntary gymnastic exercises of the sort in the country. Those participating in them would be inhaling vigorously the air of the little room, full of dust and laden with noxious emanations and tobacco-smoke. The perspiration would pour off them, but not one of them would take a bath afterwards. They would put on their clothes again, and allow the perspiration to dry on them and deposit still another cake of poisonous matter on the body, on the top of all the old layers from previous lessons. When I remarked to the most active of the gymnasts that I wondered at the constitutions they must have, not all to fail mortally ill together, he admitted that he certainly very often did feel unwell afterwards !

For Travellers

I have often heard commercial travellers and others, whose occupation obliges them to be away from home for long together, complain that they had simply no opportunity of strengthening their bodies by gymnastics or sports, and that they often came to provincial towns where it was difficult and entailed waste of time to get a bath, which, as everyone knows, one stands in special need of after a railway journey. Here I believe that " My System"will supply a want. There is no apparatus to be carried about or setup. As soon as you come from the railway station into your room at the hotel, you undress, stand on a carpet, and slap the body all over with a wet towel—or you can without any inconvenience carry a small india-rubber bath with you— dry yourself, and go through the rubbing exercises. As you are dressing again afterwards, you can wash your face, neck, hands, and feet with soap in the wash hand basin. As you see, the fatigues of the journey take the place of the exercises before the bath, but if you are staying several days in the same place you will of course go through the whole System either morning or evening.

For Fat and Thin People.

How can the same cause have two directly opposite effects ?

Don't you know the fable of the Indian who was so astonished to see the European blow warm and cold with the same mouth, first when his fingers were cold and then when the soup was too hot ?

I divide people, as far as their habit of body is concerned, into the following main classes : (1) The " soft-thin," (2) the "dry-thin," (3) the muscularly fat, (4) the skinny, and (5) the flabbily fat. There are, of course, many intermediate stages ; for instance, one sees people who actually in the upper part of their bodies belong to the one class, and in the lower to another. The bodies of those belonging to the first class have full, long muscles, which are quite soft when in repose, the muscles of the second class are short, well marked, and often overtrained. The third class have a layer of fat above and between otherwise really good muscles, whereas the two worst classes have practically no muscles at all. It is often very difficult to classify correctly anyone with clothes on. Thus a great many men commonly come under the description of "strong" who, from a physical point of view, are no good whatever, while apparently lean men may be athletes. One and the same individual can change classes from many different causes, i.e .: if a man in Class 1 be not careful, and do not lead a healthy life, he either goes over into Class 3 or (according to his age) too soon into Class 2. Class 4, with good living, becomes Class 5, and this last again, through illness or starvation, Class 4. The models of the antique statues, both men and women, belonged to Class 1 ; of the models of the present day, the men are generally Class 2, and the women Class 5.

With sensible training (following out my directions, for instance), people of all Classes can be transformed to Class 1 (with the exception in certain cases, of those in Class 2). People in Class 4 will get muscles on their bodies and limbs, and thus grow stouter and heavier.

As far as fat people are concerned, they must first ascertain to which class they belong, as people of the fifth class must always proceed very gradually and cautiously. There exist for this class many "flesh-reducing cures," of which Banting's, Epstein's, and Oertel's are the best known.

These of course provide long lists of minute and detailed rules as to what may, or may not, beeaten and drunk. The simplest plan, however, is to take considerably less of the same sort of food as you have previously been accustomed to, so that fresh deposits of fat are not made continually, and then to remove the old fat by working on it both internally and externally, by exercise of the muscles directly under-neath, and by rubbing.

By so doing, you also strengthen the body, which is other-wise liable to grow weaker during the process of getting thin. The most fat and the most troublesome form of fat has its seat as a rule round the waist. This abdominal fat is not specially affected by walking, or even mountain climbing, cycling, or arm exercises with heavy weights, and there is no satisfaction in the wrong parts, such as the arms and legs, growing thinner. But by the help of such local muscular ex-ercises and massage round the waist, as are amply represent-ed in " My System," it melts away in a convenient and com-fortable manner.

People of the third Class can generally bear to get rid of fat quickly by long runs, sweat-baths, and rigid training. But the troublesome part of this violent method is that the fat round the waist is the last to budge, whilst it is just that that one wishes to get rid of first. So that this training, too, should be supplemented by my "Corset and rubbing exercis-es."

The most striking proofs with which I have hitherto become acquainted that "My System" will reduce superfluous fat are the following : —A student in the Polytechnic at Zurich found himself after nine months to have lost weight to the extent of 20 kilograms = 44.1 lbs. ; an Austrian engineer reduced his weight in an even shorter period of time from 113 kilograms (249.165 lbs.) to 95 kilograms (209.475 lbs.). But far more extraordinary is the case of Signor Contini, Director of the Maison Alexandre, in Rome, who in two years, solely by the daily practice of "My System," actually reduced his weight from 123 kilograms (270 Ibs.) to 78 kilograms(171 lbs.)—a loss of no less than 99 lbs. All three at the same time found that their capacity for work and their vitality had immensely increased. Besides which, it may be seen any day how people gain 2 to 2 1/2 inches in chest circumference while at the same time losing just as much in waist measurements.

General Remarks on the Application of "My System."

It will be explained later on, in the description of the separate exercises, how beginners and more advanced workers, of different degrees of strength and according to age, should go about the same. Attention is drawn to the advice given to beginners on p. 80, and to the table concerning the different degrees of difficulty with which each exercise may be performed, on p. 88. If sufficient attention be paid to these matters, the system will be found suited to practically all, irrespective of age or sex. People suffering from acute illness, or from such grave organic defects as heart disease, cavities in the lungs, or ulceration of the bowels, must, of course, be excepted, and should in any case ask their doctor—that is, if the latter has any real, practical sympathy with Physical Culture——as to which exercises they had better omit. Even should there be something lacking in
one part, one may very well endeavour to give greater powers of resistance to the rest of the body.
It stands to reason that women, at certain times, should omit the regular bath and the exercises demanding most

exertion, and should content themselves with the easiest of the rubbing exercises.

DESCRIPTION OF THE EXERCISES

EXERCISE No. 1.

Stretching of the whole body, and arching of chest, standing. Swinging of the trunk in a circle, first round one way, then in the opposite direction.

In the morning : Out of bed ! Trousers or pyjamas (or knickerbockers) and sandals on ! Beginners should put on their stockings and bedroom slippers. —In the evening, or when changing clothes in the course of the day: Undress! except for shirt (or chemise) and the above-mentioned articles of clothing. Unbutton collar in any case, and have nothing tight round the waist or elsewhere !

Before beginning the exercises proper, stretch and strain the body, shoulders, and arms with all your might, raising the latter above your head and interlacing the fingers, the wrists being curved, which will enable you better to stretch the elbow and shoulder joints. It will not hurt for the joints to crack a little. Instead of stretching, you can " make a span " as it is called, by standing with your back to a wall, so that the heels are about 18 inches from the wall. Stretch out the arms to the sides, force them at the same time well back and turn the palms upwards. Then bend the trunk backwards till the tips of the fingers touch the wall. During this leaning back, arch the chest as much as you possibly can (but do not stick out the chin). This arching of the chest can be accentuated by rising on the balls of the feet. People who are supple in the back and shoulders ought to raise the arms above the head instead of stretching them out to the sides. In place of these introductory movements, strong people can make a " bridge " while still lying in bed. Bend the neck right back, draw the feet up under you, and, supporting your weight on the crown of your head and the soles of your feet, form an arch with your body.

Now for the exercise proper. Plant your feet firmly, to preserve your balance, about 18 inches apart (from centre to centre), with the toes turned slightly out in a natural position. With arms raised, lean the trunk over backwards (see Fig. a) and swing it with an even, circling motion towards the left (see Fig. b), and round to the front (see Fig. c)—being careful to keep the spine straight when leaning forwards, and not to face a different way—then on round to the right (see Fig. d) and to the back again (see Fig. a) until the body is once more in the same position as when you started. You must not however stop, but go on swinging or circling the trunk in wide circles, 5 times round the same way, the arms being held all the time close against the ears —a thing one is especially prone to forget while swinging forward. Then stop, and swing the trunk in the opposite direction, that is, backwards, to the right, then round to the front, towards the left, etc. : completing 5 circles.

The body in this manner moves, as it were, in the shape of an inverted cone, the apex of which is between the hips while the interlaced fingers follow the circular outline of the base.

If you have a tendency to giddiness, do not lean your head backwards when the body is swung round to the back. Otherwise it looks better for the head to follow the movements of the body. Beginners and delicate people should place the hands on the hips, and later on behind the head, instead of raising the arms. Do not forget to draw your breath evenly, through the nose, inhaling as you describe the back half of the circle and exhaling as you swing round the front.

Fig. *a*.   Fig. *c*.

Fig. *b*.   Fig. *d*.

Respiratory Exercises.

To stand up and without any previous physical exertion take long breaths — as is often recommended, especially in German books — is unnatural and absurd, in fact may positively cause derangement in the relative pressure of the vessels of the body, and produce giddiness.

Naturally also when you are going to do respiratory exercises, a need for more air should be felt, for which reason these same exercises are in their proper place only after a corresponding exertion of the body, while they, at the same time, have the important task of re-establishing the regular beating of the heart.

I have therefore introduced into "My System," wherever fit, an exercise consisting of one or more deep respirations (see time-table). While drawing as deep a breath as possible, through the nose, rise on the toes and lean the head a little back (see Fig. b). As you exhale,—also as deeply and powerfully as possible, and avoiding all jerks — lower the heels and chin (see Fig. a). While inhaling, rest the hands on the hips, holding the elbows well out from the sides so that you can expand the chest sideways : this will best enable you to fill the lungs. Although perhaps this statement is not in accordance with prevalent opinion, it can be proved by testing with a spirometer or a tape-measure. You can fill the lungs better by also raising the shoulders slightly,—which is practical, if not æsthetically beautiful ; and remember that raising and lowering the shoulders is in itself a good muscular exercise. After Exercises 2, 6, and all the rubbing exercises, you may, while inhaling, raise the arms in an outstretched position, to a level with the shoulders, holding them somewhat back (see Fig. e), and then, when exhaling, drop them again (see Fig. d), by doing which the respiratory exercises have the additional advantage of ensuring a good carriage. Delicate people can omit the heel-raising part of the exer-

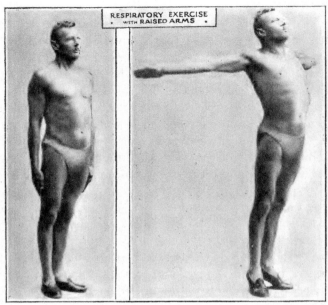

Fig. *d*.

Fig. *e*.

Fig. *f*.

cise at first, or can support themselves with one hand, as in Exercise No. 9.

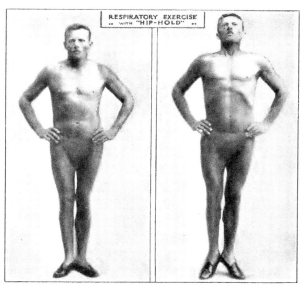

Fig. *a.*   Fig. *b.*

Fig. *c.*

Those more advanced are recommended in every 12 seconds pause to combine the two deep respirations and the raising of the heels with the deep knee-bending, as follows. Rise on the toes simultaneously with the first inhalation (Figs. b and e), sink the knees as low as you can, as you exhale the first time (Figs. c and f), straighten the legs again with the second inhalation (Figs. b and e), and finally, drop the heels simultaneously with the second exhalation (Figs. a and d). The breathing should be the main thing in your thoughts all the time, the bending and stretching of the legs becoming thus chiefly an accentuation of your deep inhaling and exhaling.

It is also a good plan, every time you sink down with arms stretched, to clench the hands with all your might, this figuratively suggesting that at that particular moment all the air is to be pressed out of the lungs (see Fig. f). It is at the same time an excellent piece of finger gymnastics, which will supplement the finger gymnastics mentioned in No. 8.

There are many other more artificial ways of breathing; I have here only indicated the most natural.

You should not unduly shoot the chest forward while actually inhaling, but it is an excellent exercise to raise or arch the chest by muscular force and keep it for a time in this position, drawing your breath by moving what in daily parlance is called the stomach, in and out. Another capital piece of lung gymnastics, recommended by the philosopher Plato and later by Kant, is to take a full respiration, and hold your breath for about a minute. One can well amuse oneself with these two chest exercises in a very practical way when out for walks by oneself, but the latter of them can only be recommended to persons with a strong heart.

Fig. *a.*

Fig. *c.*

Fig. *b.*

Fig. *d.*

EXERCISE No. 2.

71

Alternate forward and backward kick, with outstretched leg, first with one leg, then with the other.

Resting one hand on the bed-post, or the end of the bed, a heavy chair or a door-handle, and leaning the weight on one leg, strike out with the other leg 16 times backwards and forwards alternately. The free hand may be placed on the hip.

I do not mean that the leg is to be swung backwards and forwards in long strokes like a pendulum which swings of its own weight. On the contrary, the kicks should be short and sharp (see Figs. a and b), and strength should be exerted every time the movement is reversed, which ought to occur instantaneously, without a pause. The greatest strength should be concentrated on the back kick, for which reason it is most convenient to count then. If you feel afterwards that the bottom of the big muscle of the back is a little swollen, the exercise has been carried out properly. Only the last three times should you swing as far up, backwards and forwards, as you can, to render the joints and the muscles supple (see Figs. c and d). The knee should be perfectly straight all the time, and the body must not lean forward, neither must the head. If you have a footstool, stand upon it, as you can then straighten the instep too.

Then turn round and kick 16 times with the other leg. The more practised one gets, the faster this movement is performed, and it will then be found by degrees that it can be a very great exertion ; and on this account particular care must be taken that the ordinary pace of deep respiration be not increased.

EXERCISE No. 3.

Alternate raising of the upper part of the body from a re-
cumbent position, with the back of the head on the floor,
and returning to same position.

Place a footrug (or small mat) in front of the chest of drawers or wardrobe. Lie down on the mat and put your toes under the article of furniture (Fig. e). (If you do not get a firm
hold for your feet in this way, the exercise is liable to be
scamped ; in any case you do not get much proper work for
the abdominal muscles.) Raise the trunk 12 times into a
sitting position well forward (Figs. d and c), and lower it
again the same number of times (Fig. e). The back should be
held rigid and the head inclined backwards at the very last
moment, so that only the back of the head and perhaps the
fingers, but not the back or the shoulders, rest on the floor.
So long as you are weak and unpractised, it is permissible to
rest on the entire back, and in raising or lowering the body
you can make your task easier by putting your hands on the
floor, one on each side of the body.
By degrees, as the abdominal muscles grow stronger, place
the hands on the hips (Figs. a and b), and later on use the
arms to make the exercise more difficult, and consequently
more effective, putting the hands behind the neck, or holding them straight up, in a line with the body, which increases the weight of the body's leverage. You must not here
commit the serious mistake of raising the arms and bringing
them forward sooner than the body, but you should keep the
arms close to the ears (Fig.d). When you have really practised it well, it can be performed seated on a foot-stool, a
stool, or a chair (see Fig. f), by which means one is compelled to lean further over backwards, before being able to
touch the floor with the back of the head.
You do not need to keep the legs straight, the exercise being

nearly equally effective with bent knees.

Inhale as you lean back, exhale as you rise. To avoid closing the larynx, the neck should only be bent back at the last moment after inhaling.

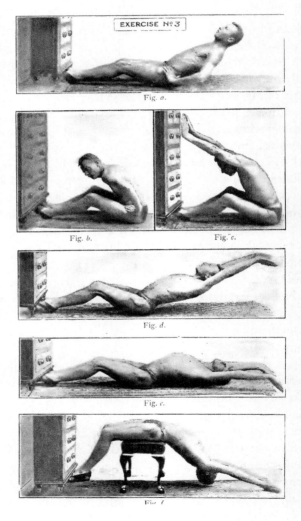

Fig. *a.*

Fig. *b.*   Fig. *c.*

Fig. *d.*

Fig. *e.*

Fig. *f.*

EXERCISE No. 4.

Complete trunk-twisting in alternate directions each time followed by "side-bending" to the side opposite to that towards which the body has been twisted, the arms meanwhile held outstretched, in a line with the shoulders.

Stand firmly, with legs wide apart, the toes pointing straight out, or a trifle inwards (with a space of about 20 to 25 inches from the middle of the one foot to the middle of the other, somewhat less for short people). Stretch the arms straight out to the sides, and close the fists (Fig. a). Turn the body a quarter round (90°) to the left, without the feet moving, and without the relative position of the arms being altered (Fig. b). You then have the "ready" position for this exercise, which fails naturally into a measure of three beats.

1st beat: Whilst standing in this turned or twisted position, bend the body down to the right sideways, till the clenched hand touches the floor between the feet (Fig. c) (first beat). Only a very few, however, can do this without bending the right knee somewhat when the hand meets the floor inside the right foot.

2nd beat : As soon as you have touched the floor, raise the body again, and—without changing front—remain standing again for a moment in the "ready" position (Fig. b).

3rd beat : Now, the feet remaining in the same place, twist the trunk half round to the right (180°), so that the face is turned in the same direction as the back of the head was before. The position for that matter is an exact replica, only reversed, of the "ready" position (see Fig. d). Then repeat the threefold movement, but in the opposite direction, first bending the trunk down to the left, and touching the floor with the left hand inside the left foot (now the left knee may be slightly bent), then raise the trunk again (Fig. d) and finally twist it back into the "ready" position (Fig. b), when

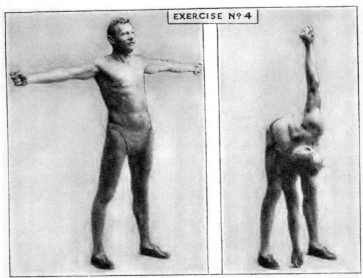

EXERCISE Nº 4

Fig *a.*

Fig. *c.*

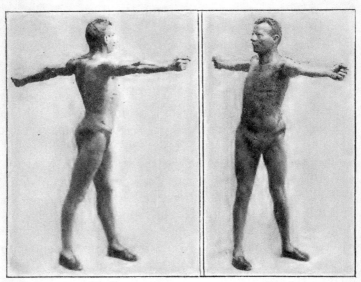

Fig. *b.*

Fig. *d.*

76

the threefold movement should be repeated for the third time, this time exactly like the first, and so on alternately.

As soon as you have learnt the movement, leave off counting 3 and count only the number of complete movements, which is done most readily by counting each time you put your hand upon the floor. There is time allowed for 10 complete movements. When you have grown stronger, through doing the exercise, you ought to give a powerful jerk or toss with the 2nd and 3rd beats (that is, with the rising and the twisting), but the " side-bendings " must always be done quietly. Do not forget to breathe evenly through the nose, inhaling with the 2nd and 3rd beats, exhaling during the "side-bending."

This exercise, together with No. 7, forms the best gymnastics imaginable for the liver. It is also splendid for preventing diseases of the kidneys.

Delicate persons and beginners may at first omit the "side-bendings" towards the floor, likewise be satisfied with turning 10 times from one side to the other, and if there be any feeling of tiredness in the arms and shoulders, they may also drop the arms, every time they turn.

EXERCISE No. 5.

Swinging the arms round in small circles, first in one direction and then the opposite direction. with the body in the "lunge" position, first with the left foot forward then with the right.

Advance the left foot 30 to 36 inches in front of the right, bending the left knee, as if to make a lunge in fencing, and hold the arms out sideways, palms uppermost. Then drop the hands about 6 inches (see Fig. a) and begin to swing them—palms uppermost—up to the front and down to the back, in circles the diameters of which should not exceed 12 inches. The last 3 circles only should, for the sake of the shoulder-joints, be as large as possible (Figs. b and c).

Each arm thus moves in the shape of a cone lying on its side, the apex of which is in the shoulder-joint, while the finger-tips follow the outline of its base.

As soon as you have made 16 circles, or air-cones, draw the left foot back, lunge with the right foot forward, turn the palms downwards, raise the hands 6 inches and now swing them 16 times forward (Fig. e), down to the front (Fig. d), and up to the back, etc. : that is, reversing the former direction.

The stronger you get, the bigger lunges must be made, and the faster you should swing the arms round, but the circles, except the 3 last each time, should not be larger.

This method of swinging the arms is much better for developing the muscles than the customary method, in wide circles, in which latter the weight of the arms themselves provides a considerable proportion of the swinging force. You can prove this for yourself by swinging the one arm by itself, and with the other hand feeling all the muscles round the armpit and the shoulder.

The exercise is rendered more effectual for the back, if somewhat more difficult, by allowing the body to lean forward, in a line, as it were, with the hindmost, outstretched leg. But be careful to force the arms well back while describing the circles. It might be advisable for those who are considerably advanced to describe these circles lying face downwards with the thighs resting on a pillow, hassock, or stool,
the toes under the wardrobe or chest of drawers, or the feet under the bed. The body should be raised from the waist upwards, the back hollowed and the shoulders forced well back. During the performance of the quick movements of this exercise also, quiet and deep breathing is essential.

EXERCISE No. 6.

Circling of legs, first swinging the legs round in one direction, then the opposite, in both instances pressing the feet together when they meet.

Lie down on your back on the rug, or upon a couch, the hands resting on the hips, or else the arms at the sides and the hands flat on the floor. Raise the legs, perfectly straight and close together, a good foot from the ground (Fig. a), then swing the feet, the instep kept straight, in circles up and outwards, the left foot to the left, and the right to the right (Fig. b), then down (Fig. c) and together again (Fig. a), and so on, 8 times round altogether, the first 6 times in circles of 2 feet diameter (rather less for short persons). When the feet meet after a completed circuit press them firmly together. Each leg thus describes, as it were, the shape of a cone lying on its side, with its apex in the hip-joint, while the toes follow the outline of the base. The two last circles should be as large as possible, and the feet of course should then cross one another instead of meeting (see Figs. d and

EXERCISE Nº 5

Fig. *a.*

Fig. *d.*

Fig. *b.*

Fig. *e.*

Fig. *c.*

Fig. *f.*

80

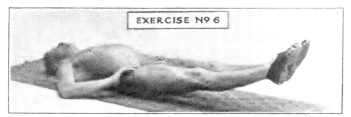

EXERCISE Nº 6

Fig. *a.*

Fig. *b.*

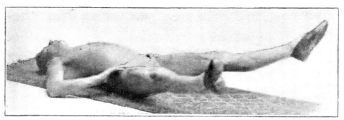

Fig. *c.*

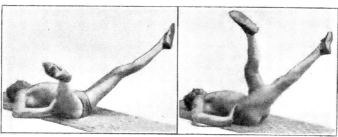

Fig. *d.*   Fig. *c.*

e).

Then swing the legs in a similar manner 8 times round the reverse way. Thus, starting from their point of contact, the left foot should be lowered in a curve to the left, the right lowered in a curve to the right, both out to the sides, up, and in a curve towards one another until they meet, to be separated again when the next circuit commences.

People who are not strong should be content, at first, to swing one leg at a time,1 or they may let their feet rest upon the floor after each circuit. The exercise may also be made easier (but of course at the same time less effective) by putting the hands behind the neck, or resting them under the thighs, or by lying with the head in front of a cupboard or a chest of drawers, so that you can bring your arms behind, and with the fingers lay hold of the article of furniture from underneath. This exercise develops strong abdominal muscles, and acts upon the digestive organs. The stronger one grows the more slowly ought these leg circlings to be performed.

Do not forget to breathe evenly through the nose. Exhale while the feet are lowered and pressed together, inhale the rest of the time.

EXERCISE No. 7.

Standing with trunk twisted round, lean forward, over to alternate sides, each time following this up by twisting round in the opposite direction from that in which the "forward leaning" has last taken place, the arms meanwhile being held straight out in a line with the shoulders.

Take up the " ready " position described in Exercise 4 (see Fig. a of Exercise, No. 7). With back straight and head thrown well back, lean the trunk, facing towards the left, forward over the left leg, the left knee being slightly bent. You thus have the preliminary position for this exercise (Fig. b). Now twist the trunk round to the right (an angle of 180°) so that the left hand is exactly where the right was before. The trunk is thus in precisely the same place over the left leg, but turned the other way, bent backwards and with face upwards (Fig. c). Continuing to face to the right, raise and move the trunk out over the right leg, until you find yourself in a position exactly corresponding to the above-mentioned preliminary position (Fig. d).

You then twist the trunk right round again, but this time, of course, to the left (see Figs. e and f). The trunk then leans again, with front to the left, over the left leg (Fig. b), twists round to the right (Fig. c) and for the second time moves over to the right side (Fig. d), and so on alternately, from one side to the other.

This exercise thus fails into a measure of 2 beats only. The one is perpetually a complete twist of the trunk, and the other a raising and "forward leaning" to the side. When you know the exercise you count once only with each complete movement, either with the " twisting round " or the "forward leaning."

Time is allowed for 10 twists, 5, that is, over the left leg, and 5 over the right.

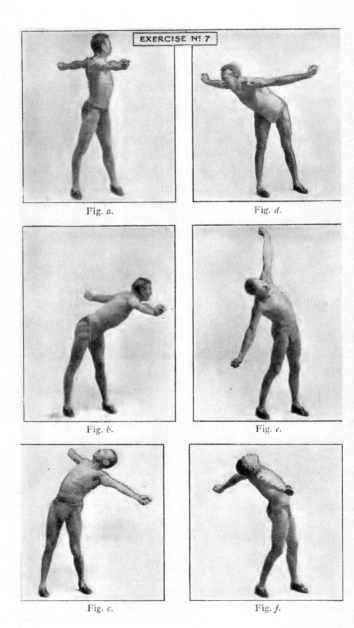

EXERCISE N.º 7

Fig. a.

Fig. d.

Fig. b.

Fig. e.

Fig. c.

Fig. f.

During the whole of the exercise the feet should remain quite stationary, with the toes pointing straight out, or rather, a little turned in. The arms, as in Exercise 4, should be held straight out the whole time in a line with the shoulders and each other, and the fists should be clenched. You inhale best during the "twisting," and exhale while raising and "forward leaning."

This exercise provides the best means of keeping the vertebral column supple, and the spinal cord and principal nerve centres fresh and active.

Delicate people and beginners may commence by raising the body from the "forward-leaning" position without twisting round, thus always waiting to twist until the body has regained its upright posture. If there be any feeling of tiredness in the arms or shoulders, drop the arms each time you lean to either side.

Strong and very advanced people can do the twisting in one jerk, but the rising and forward leaning, during which the breath is exhaled, must always be carried out comparatively quietly.

EXERCISE No. 8.

Alternate bending and straightening of the arms, lying face downwards, the weight resting on the hands and toes. Thereafter a back exercise.

Lay yourself face downwards on the carpet, in such a manner that your weight only rests on the toes and the palms of the hands (Fig. c). The hands should be just about under the shoulders, with the finger-tips pointing forwards or a little inwards, and the body should be kept straight and rigid, so that you neither stick out the seat, nor let the stomach sink down towards the floor. Keeping the body and legs rigid, and in a straight line, bend the arms (Fig. d) until the head touches the floor (Fig. e), when the arms should at once be straightened again (Fig. c). Sink the body once more, and raise it again, and continue in this manner, in even cadence, 12 times. The head should be turned sideways, alternately to right and left, on every sinking of the body.

You ought to inhale when bending the arms, and exhale when straightening them.

Delicate people may, at first, rest on the hands and knees, as well, and should not bend their arms more than will allow them to rise again with ease ; or they may perform the exercise standing, resting the hands against the edge of the chest of drawers, a heavy chair (Figs. a and b), or a window-sill, while bending and stretching the arms, which is considerably easier than carrying out the exercise on the floor.

The exercise can be rendered more difficult by raising one leg, with ankle and knee rigid, every time you lower yourself by the arms (Fig. f). Raise the right and the left leg alternately. When you are still stronger, rest on the finger-tips alone (Fig. f), instead of on the whole hand. The exercise thus becomes a very effective piece of finger gymnastics as well.

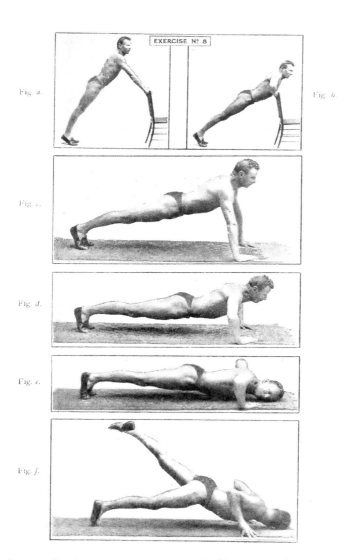

Fig. a. Fig. b.

Fig. c.

Fig. d.

Fig. e.

Fig. f.

Just as the 8 exercises were preceded by a stretching or arching of the body, standing, they may very fitly be concluded
with a similar stretching, or "back exercise," lying down, as

follows. Lower the body till the whole of it is resting on the floor face downwards, stretch the arms forward (up above the head) and the legs, with outstretched instep, straight out to the back. Then lift both the body (from the waist) and the legs, with knee straight, from the floor, the back curved inwards as much as possible, whereby the body—after some little practice—comes to form an arch like the rocker of a rocking-horse, only the " stomach " resting on the floor. Remain some few moments in this position.

The Bath, as it may be arranged in houses without special bathroom.

The middle part of the preceding longer interval may be utilised to put the little flat "sponge-bath" and water-can ready on the floor. The simplest plan is to use an ordinary wash hand basin and jug ; the best and most practical thing, however, is to make use of a hand shower-bath and an ordinary bucket. If you do not like absolutely cold water, which is best for the nervous system, so long as one does not suffer from "nerves," you can fill the can some time beforehand, for instance, in the evening, if you are taking your bath in the morning, and let the water stand in the room over night. The hand shower-bath is easily filled by dipping it in the full bucket. The bath will be more strengthening and refreshing if you put a handful of common salt into the water, giving it time to melt.

The bath itself can, of course, be taken in different ways. Some are in the habit of taking a large sponge, dipping it in the water, and squeezing it over themselves. I will describe the most practical mode of procedure.

Stand up in the middle of the "sponge-bath," and pour the contents of the sprinkler over yourself. Then sit down in the middle of the bath, and pour the rest of the water in the bucket over you. With a little practice you can manage so that the water divides and runs down the body, without any worth mentioning being spilt. But be careful not to make water-jets of your elbows. If it be absolutely necessary that not a drop shall be spilt, you should sit down straight away, before beginning to wet yourself. But even if you are standing up, you need not upset more water than if you were sprinkling the floor for sweeping,—and that is a good thing to do.

Then lie down on your back in the bath, which will cause the volume of water to rise, so that by rolling a little over on the sides you can get both arms and sides under water. Scoop the water up from the sides, first in one hand, then in the other, to get it up to the front parts of the body that the water cannot reach. Then situp, well back in the bath, and pour water some few times down the sides of the chest, forming a cup with the two hands. Afterwards pour water in the same way over the upper and under side of the thighs, then bathe the seat, and finally stand up again and wash the lower part of the legs and the feet.

On a Saturday, when you have used warm water and soap, swill yourself all over afterwards with cold water, using a jug or hand shower-bath.

After use, it is very little trouble to pour the whole of the contents of the bath back into the bucket.

Any maid can do it, as there will only be one bucketful of water.

Drying of the Body.

While still standing in the bath, wipe or rub yourself down a few times with the hands, with similar action to that described under Exercise II, but of course you must also rub down the front of the legs. This will get rid of most of the water. In the same way wipe the water off the arms and hair, into the bath. Then shake the water from your feet, stand on a small rug or mat 1 and begin the actual drying of the body with a towel. First dry your hair, face, and neck, so that the water shall not drip from them on to your body whilst you are drying that. Next rub the front of the body, several times up and down from the neck to the abdomen, and several times up and down the sides from the armpits to below the hips. The best way of doing this is to fold the towel double round the one open hand, while you hold both ends of it in the other hand (see Fig. a).

Fig. *a*.

Then comes the turn of the shoulders and the back. Fling the towel over the one shoulder, take hold of each end with one hand, and work up and down with both hands alternately, so that the back gets dried obliquely (see Fig. b). But, at the same time, slide the towel along sideways, so that by degrees the back gets rubbed several times over from the edge of the one shoulder to the other and back again. Then pass the upper end of the towel over the head so that it now rests on the other shoulder, change hands (that is, the hand that was uppermost before should now be undermost) and repeat the process, the direction of the movement crossing the first in an X.

Fig. b.

The life-size statue of the Author, made by the Danish sculptor Boegebjerg.

91

Then let the top end of the towel slide down over the shoulder and arm, and alter your grasp of that end, so that the towel is now held as shown in Fig. c. By now passing it quickly backwards and for-wards, pulling with each hand alternately, nearly the whole of the back gets rubbed, from the loins up to as high as you can reach, and then in zig-zag right down to the heels, and up again to the loins.

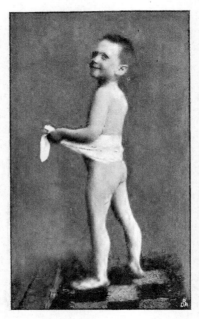

Fig. *c.*

Ib, the Author's eldest son, at the age of 4½ years.

After this dry the hands and arms with the help of the movements described in Exercise 10 (the towel must of course be held between the open hand and the skin). If you have a tendency to cold arms—which is often the case with men who wear long-sleeved woollen vests, whereas women rarely feel the cold in their arms—they can be dried before the body. Then dry between the legs, and after that the fronts and sides of the legs. Lastly dry the feet, first one, and then the other, and you should habituate yourself to doing this standing on one leg like a stork, which constitutes a very good balancing exercise. The soles of the feet are best dried by taking one end of the towel in each hand and pulling it towards you, with each hand alternately, and while you are drying in between all the toes—there is plenty of time for that—rest your heel upon your knee. If you only set aside one quarter of an hour for physical exercise, you must certainly not sit down upon a chair to rest during the time.

People who know how to dry themselves will perhaps consider these minute directions superfluous. Still, I have seen many stand and fiddle about with the towel for several minutes without getting properly dried, even then. And I am thinking, too, of all the people who have, so to speak, never been in the position of requiring to dry themselves after a bath, because they have hardly ever done such a thing as to take one.

The Rubbing Exercises

are all performed standing, that the body may not get soiled or dusty again after the bath. As in addition to providing a stroking of the entire surface of the skin they include a number of muscular exercises for the arms, breast, and back, 4 leg exercises, 2 forward and backward bendings, 2 side bendings, and 2 trunk-twisting exercises, together with 8 breathing exercises, they form a complete whole in themselves and can very advantageously be carried out in the evening, for instance, before going to bed, if you have gone through the entire System with the bath in the morning. It is only a matter of 5 or 6 minutes. It is advisable for ladies to do the stroking of the front of the body in an upward direction, instead of from above downwards. This applies to Exer-

cises 11 and 18 (see directions in " My System for Ladies.")
The limbs, on the whole, get stroked more towards the body
than from the body, and it should also be remembered that
more strength should be put out when stroking in towards
the body. It is a good plan at first to rub a little vaseline,
lanoline, or something of the kind on the nipple of the
breast.

EXERCISE No. 9.

Rubbing of the feet, the top of the back, and round the
neck.

Rest your right hand on the bedpost, a chair, or a door han-
dle, and rub the top and side of one foot 25 times with the
other foot, the sole of which thus of course itself gets rubbed
(see Figs. a , b, c and d). At the same time rub with the left
hand the back of your neck as far as you can reach from the
top down the middle of the back (Fig. a), all round the neck
(Figs. b and c) and throat (Fig. d). Then change about and
begin the same number of rubbing movements with the opposite hand and foot. People who are inclined to get too
much blood to the head, and cold feet, ought to repeat this
exercise at the end, after No. 18; but in that case there
should certainly also be time allowed for a 12 seconds'
breathing pause between the 2 exercises. Beginners may perform the movements separately, first the rubbings with the
feet, then those with the hands.

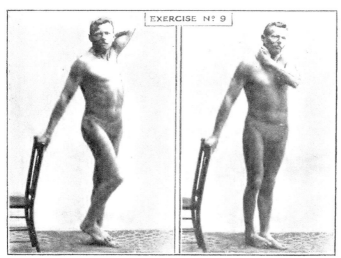

EXERCISE N° 9

Fig. *a.*   Fig. *c.*

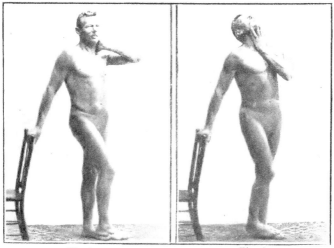

Fig. *b.*   Fig. *d.*

95

EXERCISE No. 10.

Rubbing of the arms, shoulders, and from the shoulder-blades, under the armpits, to the breast.

This exercise can be carried out best as follows : —Extend the left arm, palm downwards. With the right palm, stroke the upper side of the left arm (Fig. a) from the tips of the fingers to the shoulder and on up to the neck (Fig. b)—then back again to the finger-tips (Fig. a)—after that, in the same way, the under-arm up to the armpit (Fig. c), and then inwards across over the left breast (Fig. d) ; here the right hand relaxes its hold, immediately slapping the left shoulder-blade smartly as far back as possible, under the left arm, which at the same time is bent so that the left hand can take firm hold round the right shoulder (Fig. e). Then the right hand strokes the part from the shoulder-blade in under the left arm-pit, when it relaxes its hold, while the left hand has at the same time stroked the upper side of the right arm from the shoulder bone (Fig. f) down to the finger-tips. The arms will now be stretched out in front of you once more, and the movement is finished, the left hand resting meanwhile above the right, ready to begin an absolutely corresponding action (but replace the word right with left, and vice versa, in the above description).

It will be seen that each complete movement falls into a measure of 5 beats which, with a very little practice, will proceed mechanically and with absolute regularity and rhythm, to your counting one, two, three, four, five. In 25 seconds there should be ample time for 10 of these movements in 5 beats, using the right and the left hands alternately.

When you have really learnt the exercise, do not count with each beat, but only each complete movement, for instance, at the moment when the arms are flung across each other.

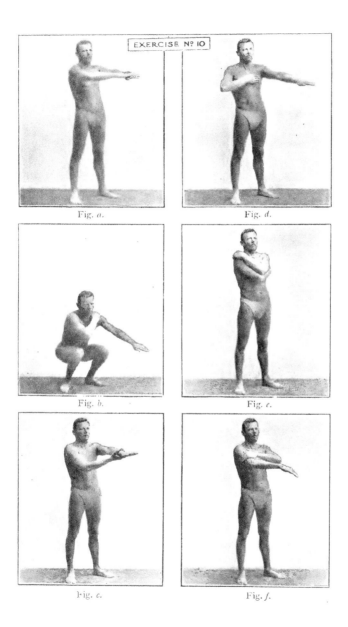

EXERCISE Nº 10

Fig. *a*.

Fig. *b*.

Fig. *c*.

Fig. *d*.

Fig. *e*.

Fig. *f*.

97

As soon as you feel sufficiently strong and capable, you can combine the exercise with 10 quick deep knee-bendings, which are performed standing on the flat sole, with a distance of from 12 to 18 inches between the feet, by which the muscles and joints of the legs are exercised in a different manner from when bending the knees, with the weight resting on the toes, and with heels close together this latter those who are more proficient can carry out simultaneously with the deep respirations. Every time you begin the stroking of the upper side of one arm, the legs should proceed to bend ; when you have crouched right down into a squatting position, you should just have reached the neck (Fig. b), and finally, see that the legs are quite straight again just as the downward stroke has finished (Fig. a). Exhale during the knee- bending, inhale all the rest of the time.

The outsides of the arms are rubbed considerably more than the insides, the skin on the back of the arms always needing it more.

When, after some little time has elapsed, the arms and shoulders have grown firm and round and the skin feels like satin—with no roughnesses on the back of the upper arm, and no wrinkles at the elbow,—you will be so fascinated by this exercise that you will increase the number of the movements of your own accord, even at the risk of exceeding the quarter of an hour. This applies both to ladies and gentlemen.

EXERCISE No. 11

Bending of the trunk, alternately backwards (distending stomach) and well forwards (drawing the stomach in), with rubbing of breast, stomach, lower part of back, loins, seat, and backs and fronts of legs, in the order given.

Legs in same position as for Exercise 1. Bend the upper part of the body well back, at the same time distending the "stomach" as much as you can, stroke with both palms, starting from the collar-bones (Fig. a), down the breast, stomach, and fore-parts of the hips (Fig. b); take your hands away, and at the same time begin to bend the trunk forward.
"stomach" should now be drawn in as much as possible, the hands meanwhile being carried round to the back, and (with thumbs pointing downward or straight out) take hold as high up above the loins as you can reach (Fig. c) and at once stroke straight down the back of the body and legs to the heels (Fig. d). You thus bring the trunk forward, with back bent, as low down as it can come, and you then, without stopping, start to raise it again, the hands passing round the insteps (Fig. e), and stroking up along the shins and the fronts of the thighs (Fig. f). Here the hands relax their hold. Swing the body over backwards again, fling your hands up once more to the collar-bones (Fig. a), and the combined movement which has just been described is gone through again from the beginning.
For women it is better not to take the hands away as they rise, but to stroke uninterruptedly from the instep up to the collar-bones (see the general remarks on the rubbing exercises, p. 64). The various movements should glide evenly over into one another, with the exception of the raising of the body, which—when you have grown stronger and have

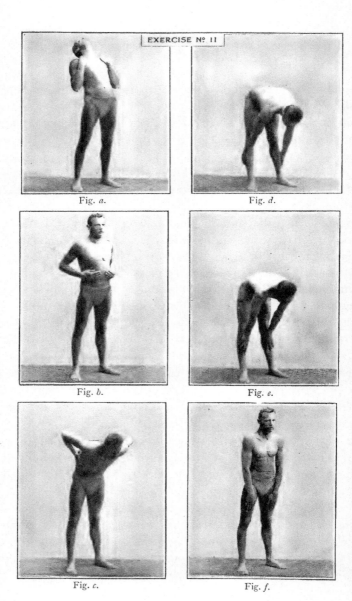

EXERCISE Nº 11

Fig. *a.*

Fig. *b.*

Fig. *c.*

Fig. *d.*

Fig. *e.*

Fig. *f.*

had more practice—should be done with a powerful jerk. Time is allowed for 20 of these complete combined movements. Every other time, or else the last 10 times, stroke up the inside of the upper part of the leg instead of up the front.

If you are not very supple, you may bend your knees a little at first, when bending forward ; later on the legs should be kept rigid all the time. A deep inhalation and corresponding exhalation should be taken during each complete movement. Inhale while rising and bending backwards, exhale when bending forwards. Do not forget the special movements of the abdomen, which are in the highest degree beneficial to the intestines.

Taking it all together, this is a splendid exercise. Edw. B. Warman, the well-known American professor, calls it "his own medicine," and has taken it every morning for many years, even when in a sleeping-car, or ship's cabin. I consider I have greatly enhanced the effectiveness of the exercise by adding the rubbing, and the distending and contracting of the "stomach."

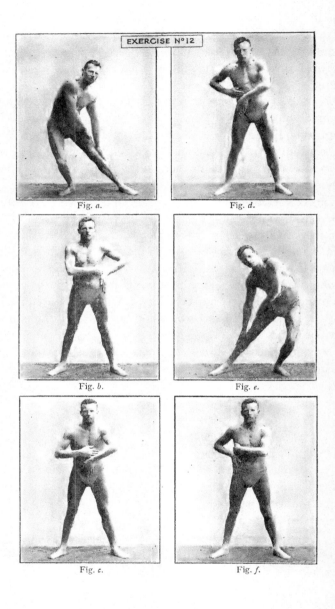

EXERCISE N°12

Fig. a.

Fig. d.

Fig. b.

Fig. e.

Fig. c.

Fig. f.

EXERCISE No. 12.

Trunk-leaning to alternate sides with corresponding stretching of the one leg and bending of the other, while rubbing successively the outer surface of the upper part of the leg the lower side of trunk, and across the stomach and the region of the diaphragm.

Legs in same position as for Exercise 4, but with the toes turned slightly out. Bend right knee, keep left leg perfectly rigid and lean the trunk as far as you can to the left. Place both palms firmly on the outer side of the left leg as far down as you can reach without stooping (Fig. a). Then, while bringing the body back into its upright position and straightening the right leg, slide your palms up the outer side of the left thigh, hip, and half up the side of the body (Fig. b), and thence across the front while the left hand is stroking the "stomach" sideways, the right is doing the same over the diaphragm (Figs. c and d).

Then take both hands away and slap them smartly down on the outer side of the right leg, the upper part of the body leaning to the right and the left knee being bent (Fig. e), whereupon the whole movement is continued in the same way (Fig. f) as described above (only with substitution of the word " left " for " right," and vice versa). Lean 8 times to each side alternately, making 16 leanings in all.

Inhale briskly each time the body is straightened (from either side) and exhale evenly the rest of the time.

It is a serious mistake to bend the trunk obliquely forward instead of leaning straight to the side. Beginners are also prone to cross their hands or to stretch the wrong knee ; it must be the knee on the side towards which the body leans.

By pressing heavily with the hands over the stomach, the intestines are well massaged. The exercise constitutes, moreover, an effective means of reducing all superfluity of fat.

EXERCISE No. 13.

Trunk-twisting half round to alternate sides, together with swinging of the arms and downward pressure with the one hand while the back of the other hand rubs the back and loins.

Stand in front of a chest of drawers, not too low, a wash-hand-stand, or other piece of furniture, at such a distance that you can comfortably reach the object without overmuch stretching forward. Feet in same position as for Exercise 1.

Swing your right arm, which should be perfectly straight out, in a wide circle starting from below, backwards (Fig. a) and upwards over to the front and down again, and at the same time twist the body (from the waist upwards) an angle of 60° (or 1/6 of a circle) to the left. The right hand, with palm downwards, has in the meantime descended upon the above-mentioned object, against which you exert a strong pressure with your outstretched arm, partly downwards, partly in towards yourself (Fig. b).

The pressure should last just as long as it takes you to rub three times backwards and forwards across the back in a zigzag from as high up as you can reach, down over the loins, with the back of the left hand (see Figs. b and c). Then take away the right hand and swing the left forward in a wide circle from the back, at the same time twisting the body round to the right, when you press with the left hand exactly as you did before with the right, the turn of which it now is to rub the back (Figs. d, e and f). There is time for 16 such half-twists, 8 to each side.

You ought to press in such wise that all the muscles round the arm- pit and in front of the trunk are on the strain. There is no better exercise on land than this for strengthening the muscles of the upper part of the body and the arms, which one uses in fast swimming. The measure, or time, of

EXERCISE № 14

Fig. *a.*

Fig. *b.*

Fig. *c.*

Fig. *d.*

Fig. *e.*

Fig. *f.*

your breathing ought also to be the same as when in the water : exhale every time you press down and in towards yourself with one hand and inhale during the arm-swinging.

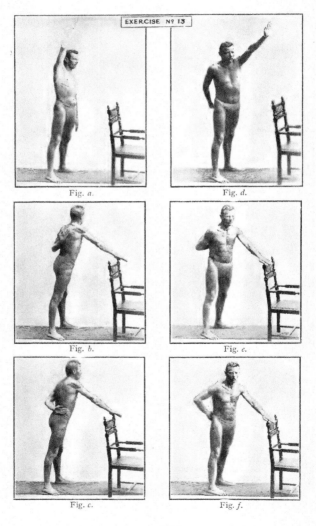

EXERCISE Nº 13

Fig. a.

Fig. d.

Fig. b.

Fig. e.

Fig. c.

Fig. f.

EXERCISE No. 14.

Alternate raising of the legs, sideways, with rubbing of the sides of the trunk and thighs.

Stand upright with heels together and palms resting against the flanks, with the fingers pointing downwards (Fig. a).
While the one leg is being lifted sideways, and as high as possible, with knee and ankle rigid, the corresponding hand strokes down the outer side of the thigh, and by so doing exerts pressure against the upward movement of the leg, by which means the muscles of the hips in particular obtain vigorous exercise (Fig. b). When the leg is dropped again, immediately after, the hand strokes upwards, but this time on the inside of the thigh (Fig. c), and the arm goes over the right groin and remains bent, while the other leg and the other arm work in their turn (Figs. e and f). There is time allowed for 20 leg-raisings, 10 with each leg. While moving the one leg, inhale ; and exhale while moving the other, and continue in like manner. This exercise develops most of the muscles of the body, and of the arms and legs as well. It is at the same time an excellent balancing exercise.

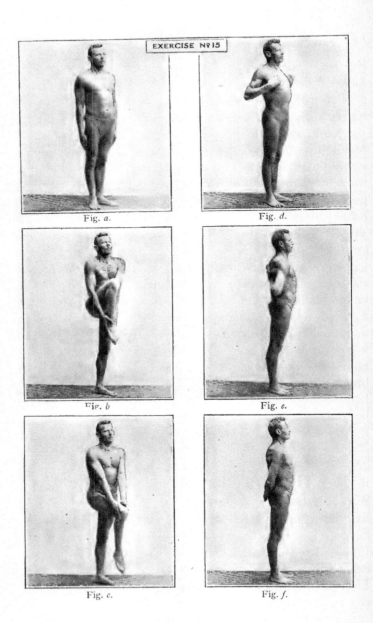

EXERCISE Nº 15

Fig. *a.*

Fig. *d.*

Fig. *b*

Fig. *e.*

Fig. *c.*

Fig. *f.*

108

EXERCISE No. 15

Raising of right and left knee alternately, and at the same time rubbing of the outer and inner sides of the lower part of the legs, followed each time by rubbing of the front and back of the body.

Stand at " attention" (Fig. a). Lift the one knee as far up towards the chest as you can without bending the body forward. The lower part of the leg should be held in a vertical position, and the instep in a straight line with the leg. Take hold of the sides of the heel with both hands (see Fig. b), and stretching the leg down again, slide the hands, one on each side, along the ankle, calf, knee, and a little way above the last (Fig. c). Resume your upright position once more, and recommence the same movement with the other leg, and so on, alternately. Between each movement there is thus a moment's pause, during which you stand still, on both feet. After some time, when you are fully conversant with this, as with all the other exercises, you ought—without taking up more time altogether—to fill up these short pauses by rubbing the body in front and behind as follows : After the hands have stroked, for instance, along the right leg, they both continue to stroke further up, over the abdomen and the breast, right up to the collar-bones (Fig. d), when they slip over to the sides, and release their hold. Immediately afterwards the right hand goes round to the back and with the back of the hand strokes once down the back, loins, and seat (Figs. e and f). When you take your hands from the left leg, the front of the body is stroked as before with both hands, whereafter the back of the left hand strokes the back. Inhale with each knee-raising and while stroking the front ; exhale while stroking the back.

Eight liftings of each knee have been calculated for; that is, sixteen altogether.

Fig. *a*.　　　　　　　　　　Fig. *b*.

Fig. *c*.

110

EXERCISE No. 16.

Flinging of the trunk to right and left alternately, each hand rubbing its own side.

Stand well up, with heels together and palms resting against the hips, with the fingers pointing downwards (Fig. a). Quickly flinging the trunk over to the left, the left palm strokes down the left hip and outer side of left thigh, while the right hand is drawn up the right side of the body (see Fig. b). The trunk is then immediately flung over to the right, while the left hand is drawn up the left side, and the right strokes down its own side (Fig. c); and so on, in the same manner (Figs. b, c , and b), but the jerks or " flingings " to each side following very quickly one upon another. The arms are bent in turn as much as possible every time the hand is drawn up, so that a longer stretch can be rubbed.

Time is allowed for 20 jerks altogether, half to each side.

The stronger you become, the more quickly the movements are performed and the harder the hands should be pressed against the body. But the body must be bent over as far as possible each time. It thus becomes a very vigorous exercise both for the arms and for almost all the muscles of the body, as well as for the internal organs. To begin with, the movement must be carried out quite slowly.

It is of the greatest importance that the breath be not held, which so many do when carrying out this and the two exercises following. To begin with, a full breath should be taken with each double movement, but later on several quick jerks can be gone through during a breath.

Time is allowed for 20 jerks altogether, half to each side.

The stronger you become, the more quickly the movements are performed and the harder the hands should be pressed against the body. But the body must be bent over as far as possible each time. It thus becomes a very vigorous exercise both for the arms and for almost all the muscles of the body, as well as for the internal organs. To begin with, the movement must be carried out quite slowly.

It is of the greatest importance that the breath be not held, which so many do when carrying out this and the two exercises following. To begin with, a full breath should be taken with each double movement, but later on several quick jerks can be gone through during a breath.

EXERCISE No. 17

A flinging twist of the trunk to each side in turn, and at same time rubbing across the whole of the breast.

Leg-position as in Exercises 4 and 7. With the legs so placed, you confine the twisting almost entirely to the trunk instead of allowing the legs to do it, in which latter case the greater part of the beneficial results of the exercise would be lost. Certainly it does not look well to stand with the toes pointing inwards, but we are not concerned here with gymnastic displays, but with health exercises performed without onlookers. Now twist the body (from the waist upwards) quickly round on its own axis about 90°, or in any case as far as you can to the left,—at first slowly, then more quickly— at the same time laying your hands flat on the right breast, the one above the nipple, the other just below it (see Fig. a). As you twist the body 180° round to the right, you slide your hands across the breast (Fig. b), that is, in an opposite direction to that in which the body is moving, so that the palms rest quite on the left side of the breast, when the

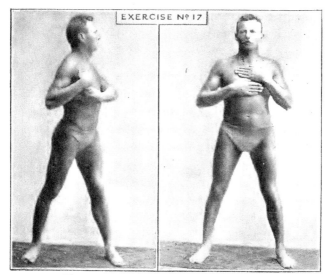

Fig. a.   Fig. b.

Fig. c.

113

twisting to the right has been accomplished (see Fig. c). Immediately afterwards bring the body round to the left again, while the hands slide back to the extreme right side of the breast (Fig. a), and continue thus, 20 times altogether, from the one side to the other alternately (Figs. c and a). The flinging of the trunk should by degrees come to be as quick as possible, and the hands must be pressed firmly against the breast. Observe that the same hand moves continually in a horizontal line, the left, for example, being above the nipple the whole time and the right below. But it is advisable to change the hands each day.

In this exercise and No. 12 the whole of the front part of the trunk gets rubbed across. The front of the trunk measures in height exactly three times the width of the hand (with fingers a little spread out) + one hand's length. These crosswise rubbing exercises are important, and not least because certain parts of the front of the body do not get worked upon by lengthways rubbing.

Beginners ought to perform this exercise gently, without jerking or flinging. It is a serious mistake to twist the head only, so that the body, from the waist upwards, remains almost stationary.

In order to be sure that you really do turn half round, or more, each time, mark a point or vertical line just behind your back, which mark should be reached, or passed, by each shoulder alternately. Breathing as in Exercise 16.

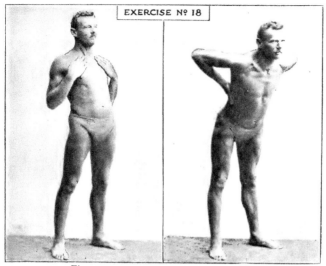

EXERCISE Nº 18

Fig. *a.*
Fig. *c.*

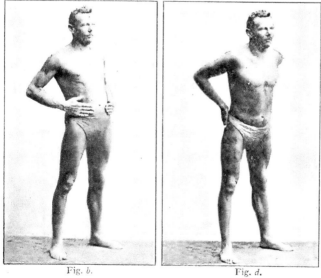

Fig. *b.*
Fig. *d.*

115

EXERCISE No. 18.

Flinging of the trunk, alternately backwards, rubbing the breast, and forwards, rubbing the loins.

Legs as in Exercise 11. First fling the trunk backwards, but not so far as in Exercise n (Fig. a). Meanwhile stroke down the breast and fronts of the hips (Fig. b) with your hands (ladies, however, the reverse, viz. : from under the breasts up to the collar-bones as described in "My System for Ladies"). Then fling the trunk somewhat forward, without curving the back or contracting the " stomach " (Fig. c). The body should be stroked on the back in the same manner as described in Exercise 11, but stop short a little way below the loins (Fig. d). The trunk is then at once flung back again into the first position, and the front stroked as before (Figs. a and b) ; then forward again, with rubbing of the back, and so on 20 jerks, following quickly one upon another, backwards and forwards alternately. Breathing as in Exercises 16 and 17. Beginners ought, of course, to perform this exercise slowly.

CONCLUSION
AND ADVICE FOR BEGINNERS.

Dear Reader !

My little book has turned out much longer than I originally intended.

I never thought that the explanations of these 15 minutes' work would take up so much space.

Still you need not alarm yourself by fancying there is anything very complicated behind these detailed descriptions. You will probably be able to do the exercises after simply reading the headings and glancing at the illustrations. But you must admit that it is well in cases of doubt to be able to ascertain how a detail may best be carried out.

Whether you are weak or strong, young or old, I advise you to begin these exercises at once, and rather to-day than to-morrow. But do not attack them too vigorously at first, unless you are accustomed to physical work. Do not delay because you do not happen to have a bath ; you can buy one when convenient, and in the meantime be content to rub yourself all over with a wet towel. Or, this very evening, do some of the rubbing exercises, for example, Exercises 11, 10, 12, and 16, with long respirations between ! By so doing you will get an air bath and a taste of the inestimable enjoyment that results from these exercises, without any fear of over-exerting yourself, or feeling tender and uncomfortable in the morning. The next few evenings you can take by degrees all the rubbing exercises, and then when you have an opportunity in the course of the day, try to do one or another of the Exercises 1 to 8, with your clothes on.

Then we will suppose that in the meantime you have procured a small tub, or flat bath. One fine morning you pull yourself together and get up 20 minutes earlier than usual, do the 8 exercises, pour some lukewarm water over yourself, dry yourself, rub yourself, dress, and— later on, during your day's work, you will be surprised and delighted to feel the refreshing sensation pervading your body all the time. Here indeed we have an application of the proverb about small causes and great effects ! If you had spent a whole hour in morning gymnastics, you would very likely have been more tired and disinclined for work than you used to be without any exercise whatever.

I purposely wrote lukewarm water, for it is pure superstition to suppose that icy cold water is the only saving thing. The essential condition is that you should directly apply water, air, and rubbing to the entire surface of your skin, and that you should find it so pleasant that you feel a need and a desire to persevere. There will then come a time when you will use the water cold simply because it is more convenient, and no longer makes you shudder. And then it will make your nerves steadier still, although it might have had just the opposite effect, to begin with, on people with highly-strung nervous systems.

Yes, it gives you a delightful feeling of satisfaction, having taken this early morning exercise and bath ! You get such a good conscience that even if later on in the day you have no time for any exercise or recreation whatever, it will not signify ; you may rest content, for you have indeed for this day done your duty to your bodily self.

Finally, have no fear that I propose to make a parody of a " strong man " out of you. I can well understand that you have a terror of getting to resemble those respectable gentlemen whose powerful physical development has proceeded in defiance of all laws of harmony and beauty. They feel called upon to round their elbows and to spread out and stick up their toes, to show how they can hardly walk for strength, and the greater the " dead weight " they can attain the better they are pleased. When they get photographed they lay themselves out to impress the beholder by forcing their unnaturally distended arm muscles into prominence, till they seem to be even more exaggeratedly developed and knotted than they are in reality; or they lean forward with sombre mien and convulsively contract all the muscles in the front of their body. Every German and English " strong man " magazine teems with repulsive pictures of the sort.

How supremely calm, how dignified and superior, and how delightfully harmonious, in comparison, the antique classical figures are ! In them you never see a muscle on the strain, unless this be called for in the position or movement represented. Everything bears the impress of perfect health and beauty : arched chest, broad and rounded shoulders, slender hips, the muscles of the trunk full, and the limbs substantial at the root but growing gradually slenderer towards the delicate wrists and insteps. It is from this company that you should select your model.

It is daily physical exercise, if only for a short time, that has so excellent an effect. It ought therefore to become a habit, a necessity that a well-ordered household can just as ill dispense with a swarm dishes for dinner or a cloth on the table. Daily exercise can by no means be replaced by, for example, one hour's gymnastics twice a week in the evening, 2 hours' practice at games or sports, however excellent the latter may be, regarded as supplementary.

Fifteen minutes every morning and 5 1/2 minutes every evening only come altogether to about 1/2 hour more in the week ; how can it be, then, that its effect on the human frame is so much greater and better ? The reason is, you see, that during an hour's gymnastics in company a great deal of time is spent in changing one's clothes, in words of command, pauses, and in watching others, in addition to which it is almost invariably the case that many of the exercises have comparatively little direct influence upon the health. These 7 short intervals of 15 + 5 1/2 minutes, on the contrary, are, from the first second to the last, filled with hard work for the most vital organs. Finally, the body can only "digest" with advantage a certain amount of gymnastics at one time ; if it gets too much in one dose, the result may be more harmful than beneficial.

When, with such thoughts in my mind, I turn to gymnastics as they are taught in schools, it seems to me that these latter are anything but adequate. In my opinion, the instruction in this branch should assist the physical development, not only during school years, but later in life as well.

In most other subjects—reading, writing, and arithmetic, for instance—the pupil acquires knowledge of which he can make daily use in after-life. The gymnastic instruction, on the other hand, requires rooms and apparatus which are not readily or daily accessible to him after he has left school.

In reality, there exist only two main forms of rational physical education for the young ; and each of these forms is supplementary to the other. Exercise in open-air sports and games constitutes the first of these methods, by which the physical and, to a high degree, the moral conditions of the young are simultaneously improved. The ideal physically developed man must be, so to speak, a supple-limbed, agile being, whose chief characteristics are activity and power of endurance, and these attributes are best attained through the medium of sports and games, a method, to be sure, not calculated to produce that ponderous muscularity as artificially developed by exercises performed with heavy weights and with various kinds of gymnastic apparatus. But such a condition is not even worth the striving for, for where practical life is concerned, such can only be regarded as a dead burden, unwieldy, superfluous, troublesome, and probably unhealthy. Moreover, open-air sports and games have the further advantage of being, at the present day, the only means of encouraging in youth such mental qualities and attributes of character as courage, resolution, presence of mind, commercial ability, feeling of good fellowship, and readiness to assist the weak.

The second main form of physical culture for the young is the prosecution of a system of home gymnastics dealing with all the organs of the body, and it must be a task of the school to make the children entrusted to its care skilful in the same and to urge them to the exercise of it.

The system must be so compiled that its use shall—in so far as it lies within human power—guarantee the maintenance of health and act as a safeguard against the majority of illnesses. The exercises, therefore, must principally and particularly have as object the promotion of the proper functional activity of the respiratory organs, the circulation, the skin, and the organs of digestion. A satisfactory development of the muscular system will result as a matter of course.

This ideal system must be indissolubly connected with the daily water-bath, air-bath, and massage, but beyond that should require no apparatus whatsoever. Above all, it should be a system which the pupils can carry out in whatsoever conditions they may encounter in after-life. The pupils must not only learn the exercises themselves in school : it must be impressed upon them that this little system must form and always remain a part of their morning (or evening) toilet. It must be capable of being performed with like benefit by the poorest as by the richest, by the weakling as by the athlete, by young and old, girls and boys, men and women. Its performance must not require more time than from 15 to 20 minutes daily, and, so as not to tax the memory, every single exercise must be so that it can be performed in exact repetition throughout life. Likewise all the exercises must be the same for all ; but, that they may be suited to different individuals, according to age, sex, or strength, each single exercise must be arranged in a number of different degrees of difficulty, i.e., easier and more difficult ways of being performed.

Public schools, grammar schools, and high schools, as well as council schools, would be in a position to develop in their pupils, to a much greater extent than is now the case, a sense of the importance of hygiene and the proper care of the body, if through such a short system of home gymnastics—mine or some other—combined daily with bath and rubbing, they accustomed them to the comforts of cleanliness and properly cared-for bodies.

A scholar who has had a physical education of this sort will really have brought out of his school experience something that will be of benefit to him his whole life through. This is the more desirable since the greater part of the physical and mental work of to-day is carried out under injurious external conditions. I am persuaded that the future will see my opinions put into practice.

Even if you are as healthy and well as you think you can be, you ought all the same to accustom yourself to a daily bath and all-round daily exercise. If you are really fortunate enough to enjoy good health, you ought to put yourself to this slight inconvenience in order to retain and increase the same, but it is only the first step that is possibly a trifle unpleasant. You will soon get so "addicted" to these rejuvenating few minutes that you would not be deprived of them at any price.

You ought to do it, not for your own sake only, but even more for the sake of your descendants, that they may not degenerate through you.

How many children of healthy parents one sees come from the country into the town, and get completely absorbed by intellectual interests. If they are "fortunate" enough to become rich, they are soon involved in a whirl of social functions, high living, all sorts of luxury, and perhaps various vices. They then come to look with contempt on the manual labour that was the source of their parents' health and strength and to which they owe it entirely that their own health is not quickly wrecked by their one-sided intellectual over-culture. But their offspring, even in the first generation, are delicate and overstrung, while their grand children stand with one foot in the grave when they are born, or, at any rate, come into the world with a ticket of admission to the lunatic asylum. And all this misery might have been avoided had they reflected in time that the body is not a mere covering, of itself of no account, for the soul and mind, but is the soil wherein all germinating power has its birth. So you must not impoverish your body, like a careless man farming rented land, but you should, like a prudent landowner, make it an object of wise and careful culture, remembering that this is an investment which yields good interest.

A body which is not daily exercised in every part, inside and out, decays, that is to say, grows decrepit and "old" before its time. There is, of course, no pleasure or advantage in growing old in years, if you are broken down, stiff, infirm, and full of ailments, with your intelligence well-nigh extinguished and your interests fled. Thus it is with no small number of people who have grown old, in spite of the fact that they have their whole life long pooh-poohed fresh air, sunlight, water, and gymnastics. The daily sight of these old wrecks has even given many young people a distaste for old age, so that they do not care in the least to do anything which will make them live long. One thus overlooks the fact that it is possible and indeed quite natural to preserve both the physical and the mental faculties almost unimpaired for at least a hundred years, and that this will mean an enormous addition to the happiness and wealth—both in money and experience—of the family, the race, and the State.

The chief advantage of rational physical exercise is thus not so much that the muscles and sinews grow stronger, as that all the internal organs, including even the brain, heart, and spinal cord, are daily cleansed in a rejuvenating bath. Do you think that a vertebral column, for instance, which is daily submitted to as many stretchings, bendings, and twistings to its utmost capacity, as is the case in " My System," can get stiff and calcinated and possibly impede the efficiency of the chief nerve-fibres which pass through it ? This is so far from being the case, that even you, dear Sir, who are already getting on in years, if you will only begin these exercises now, will be able to grow more supple, and more erect and agile, than you were as a youth ; indeed you will probably in a few months add a whole inch to your stature, as many others write to me that they have done. For this reason I would ask everyone who begins "My System" to have his height accurately measured, and likewise to measure the circumference of his chest, while the lungs are filled with air, and afterwards again when all the air has been exhaled. They can then see what the difference in the two chest measurements is after a space of six months.

All measurements of the upper and lower part of the arm, the thigh and calf, hips, waist, neck, etc., such as have to be taken in every other system, are unimportant, since they give no information regarding the shape of the muscles, still less of their substance or capabilities. A measurement of the waist, for example, does not tell how much of the body is fat and how much muscle. If you are willing to take a little trouble to ascertain your progress in an obvious and convincing manner, you ought to have your photograph taken without clothes on—and preferably with the arms held out from the body—and then after due lapse of time have a second photograph taken in the same position, of the same size, and in the same light.

It has been said in certain quarters,—and even by people who, in their own opinion, were well qualified to speak on the subject—that " My System" contains too many (some have even declared exclusively) exercises for the muscles of the abdomen.

The truth however is that " My System," quite apart from the subsidiary effect upon groups of muscles in other parts of the body, contains exercises for the muscles of the abdomen in a carefully-calculated and absolutely correct proportion.

The reason that individual critics have come forward with the above-mentioned objection is simply that all other well-known systems contain too few exercises for the abdominal muscles, and perhaps also that the critics have not themselves practically tested " My System " for any length of time.

I give below the figures, —calculated by points—according to which I selected those of my exercises which were intended to act upon the extensors of the back and the straight abdominal muscles. It will be seen that the back and front of the body are treated exactly alike. If any objection could be made, it would be that there is too little work for the muscles of the abdomen, as these latter, which act upon the internal organs, must be regarded as somewhat more important than the extensors of the back, which affect the uprightness and general carriage of the body.

Table of the different difficult degrees

with which the exercises in

" MY SYSTEM "

May be performed.

The numbers to the left of each exercise indicate the ascending degrees of difficulty with which it may be performed : No. 1, therefore, is the easiest, No. 2 somewhat more difficult, and so on. The more difficult the degree of exercise, the more powerful will be its effect on the worker.

All users of " My System," beginners and elderly people especially, are earnestly advised to perform the exercises for the first time in the first— that is, the easiest—degree, and not to undertake the more difficult until the easier degree can be performed without effort.

BREATHING EXERCISES.

1. With " hip-hold " (or raised arms) without raising the heels.
2. With " hip-hold " (or raised arms) and heel-raising.
3. With " hip-hold " (or raised arms), heel-raising, and deep knee-bending.

Exercise No. 1.

1. With " hip-hold," quietly.
2. With " neck-hold," quietly.
3. With arms raised high above head and with fingers interlaced.

Exercise No. 2.

1. Without footstool, quietly.
2. With footstool, rather quickly.
3. Without support with the hand, very quickly and vigorously.

Exercise No. 3.

1. Helping with the hands to raise and lower the body, the whole of the back resting upon the floor.
2. With " hip-hold," the whole of the back resting on the floor.
3. With " neck-hold," the whole of the back resting on the floor.

4. With outstretched arms, only the head and seat to touch the floor.
5. As fourth degree, but sitting upon a footstool.
6. As fourth degree, but sitting upon a chair or a bench.

Exercise No. 4.

1. Without side-bendings, with lowering of the arms, quietly.
2. Without side-bendings, remaining with outstretched arms.
3. With side-bendings, quietly.
4. With side-bendings, quick body-raising, and twisting.

Exercise No. 5.

1. With short lunge, arms circling quietly.
2. With long lunge, arms circling quickly.
3. With long lunge, body leaning forwards, quick circles.
4. With thighs resting upon a stool or bench, quick circles.

Exercise No. 6.

1. Circling with one leg.
2. With neck-hold, rather fast, simultaneous circling with both legs.

TABLE.

No. of Exercise.	Extensors of the Back.		Points.	The Straight Abdominal Muscles.		Points.
	— —			— —		
1	Strong	..	3	Strong	..	3
2	Medium	..	2	Weak	..	1
3	Weak	..	1	Strong	..	3
4	Medium	..	2	Weak	..	1
5	Weak	..	1	0	..	0
6	Weak	..	1	Strong	..	3
7	Strong	..	3	Medium	..	2
8	Strong	..	3	Medium	..	2
9	Weak	..	1	Weak	.	1
10	0	..	0	0	..	0
11	Strong	..	3	Medium	..	2
12	Weak	..	1	Medium	..	2
13	Medium	..	2	Medium	..	2
14	Weak	..	1	Weak	..	1
15	0	..	0	Medium	..	2
16	Weak	..	1	Weak	..	1
17	Medium	..	2	Weak	..	1
18	Strong	.	3	Strong	.	3
	Total ..		30	Total ..		30

3. With head and hands on the floor, slow, simultaneous circling with both legs.

Exercise No. 7.

1. Twisting in upright position, with lowering of the arms, quietly.
2. Twisting in upright position, remaining with outstretched arms, quietly.
3. Twisting in bent position, quietly.
4. Quick twisting in bent position.

Exercise No. 8.

1. Resting the hands upon the chest of drawers, the bed rail, or something similar.
2. With hands and knees upon the floor.
3. With only the hands and the points of the toes upon the floor.
4. As third degree, but raising the leg.
5. With only fingers and toes upon the floor, raising the leg.

Exercise No. 9.

1. Gentle rubbing of feet and neck separately.
2. Vigorous rubbing of feet and neck at the same time.

Exercise No. 10.

1. In five beats, gentle rubbing.
2. Vigorous rubbing.
3. Vigorous rubbing and deep knee-bending.

Exercise No. 11.

1. Coming to erect position quietly, gentle rubbing.
2. Coming to erect position quickly, vigorous rubbing.

Exercise No. 12.

1. Quietly, gentle rubbing.
2. With vigorous stomach massage.

Exercise No. 13.

1. Quietly, gentle rubbing.
2. With heavy pressure and vigorous rubbing.

Exercise No. 14.

1. Quietly, gentle rubbing.
2. With vigorous rubbing.

Exercise No. 15.

1. Gentle rubbing of the legs only.
2. Gentle rubbing of the legs and trunk.
3. Vigorous rubbing of the legs and trunk.

Exercise No. 16.

1. Slowly, gentle rubbing.
2. Quickly, vigorous rubbing.

Exercise No. 17.

1. Slowly, gentle rubbing.
2. Quickly, vigorous rubbing.

Exercise No. 18.

1. Slowly, gentle rubbing.
2. Quickly, vigorous rubbing.

PARTICULARS AND ADVANTAGES OF "MY SYSTEM"

1. Most systems of home gymnastics consist of body exercises alone. But with " My System " the water-bath, air-bath, and respiratory exercises are inseparably connected ; the water-bath because, differing from other systems, it is introduced in the middle of the exercises ; the air-bath because the rubbing exercises can only be performed with the body naked.

2. In many other systems deep breathing is indeed recommended, but only in general. Only in "My System" are precise directions to be found concerning the breathing exercises, here introduced between the different body exercises, which serve partly as "lung gymnastics," but partly also as means of quietening the heart-beats accelerated by each exercise. No other system contains, like "My System," fixed rules concerning inhalation and exhalation during the performance of the body exercises, and it is just this point which is of such extreme importance, especially with regard to the action of the heart.

3. Of the 18 exercises of the System, 13 are absolutely new ; namely, Nos. 2, 6, and 7, and the ten rubbing exercises. Only 5 have been adopted from various other systems, appearing here in improved form.

4. All necessity for thought concerning the performance of "My System" is reduced to a minimum. Men or women, young or old, the more or less vigorous, all perform the same exercises always, but in different degrees of difficulty. Besides this, every exercise is carried out exactly the same number of times, in contrast to most other systems, in which the exercises as well as the number of repetitions keep on changing.

5. No other system has so many quick bendings and twistings of the body ; and it is just this quickness of movement

which produces speedy development of the "muscle corset," and which exerts such an advantageous influence on the internal organs.

6. "My System" requires no particular apparatus or appliance, and can be gone through anywhere and at any time.

7. "My System" works, in a minimum of time, upon all the organs of the body in suitable proportion to the importance of the muscles, and promotes thereby, in a rational manner, the normal and harmonious development of the body.

8. " My System" concerns itself principally with the internal organs and the skin, and acts, therefore, exceptionally strongly and beneficially on the metabolism and therefore on the health.

9. "My System"is above all for the healthy, that they may maintain their health and further develop their strength and beauty; and, beyond that, it has also proved itself in many cases—such as rheumatism, disordered digestion, certain heart ailments, among others,—to be, if rightly applied, an excellent method of cure. Sick people, however, should always consult a physician, but one who himself has faith in physical exercise, before taking up the system.

MY SPECIAL EXERCISES FOR THE NECK.

These are not included in "My System," because they are not actually necessary to the health. But as it does appertain to physical beauty and a good appearance to have a well-developed neck, and as all the exercises for the neck which are to be found in other books of gymnastics only partially effect their object, and as, in the third place, it is only comparatively few who have an opportunity of going in for Græco-Roman wrestling, which specially brings the muscles of the neck and throat into play, I have appended a description of 3 exercises of mine for this purpose, by the help
of which a man or woman with a thin neck can make it strong, and 3/4 in. more in circumference, in three months.

I no longer do these exercises myself, since by dint of practising them, my neck has already become too thick and therefore apparently too short. I wear an 18 1/2 inch stand-up collar, and if a man weighing 20 stone takes hold of me by the back of my head, I can lean my head back and, without using my arms, swing him right round with his feet in the air. My trick, "the suspended anvil," is also much more a test of the strength of the neck than of that of the stomach, as I lie with the back of my head resting on one chair and my heels on another, while a couple of smiths with great sledgehammers hammer away on an anvil weighing 200 lbs. placed directly upon my stomach.

1. Bending of the head backwards and forwards.

Bend the head well down to the front and grasp the upper part of the back of the head with both hands—fingers interlaced (see Fig. a). Then, while bringing the head back, resist the movement by strong pressure with the hands. When the head has, however, slowly forced its way back, place your hands under the chin (see Fig. b) and press to prevent the bending forward of the head, and so on, backwards and forwards, from 10 to 50 times.

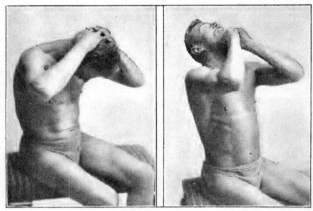

Fig. *a*.   Fig. *b*.

2. Bending of the head to the sides

Lean the head over to the right and place the left hand against the temple as shown in Fig. c. Then bend the head very slowly over to the left, pressing hard with the left hand in the contrary direction. When the head has come quite down to the left, take away the left hand and place the right hand against the right temple. The head then returns to the opposite side, the right arm resisting, and so on, in alternate directions, from 5 to 25 times.

3. Turning of the head round to the sides

Turn the head to the left, place the right hand against the right jaw, as shown in Fig. d.

Then turn the head slowly round to the right, resisting the movement by the force of the right arm. When the head is turned well to the right, take away the right hand and place the left one against the left jaw, to oppose the head turning to the left, and go on thus 5 to 25 times, first to the one side, then to the other.

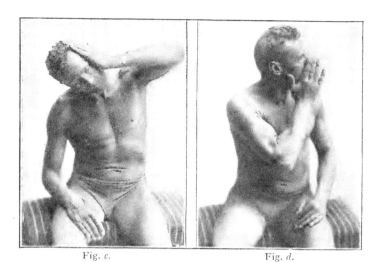

Fig. *c.*   Fig. *d.*

TIME-TABLE.

No. of Ex.	Name of Exercise.	Number of times repeated.	Time in seconds.			Explained on p.
			For Beginners.	Those more advanced.	Those in good practice.	
1	Stretching of body, then trunk circling, all standing	10		35	25	41
	Breathing-pause with raising of the heels and deep knee-bending [1] . .			12	12	
2	Backward and forward kick, standing .	2 × 16		20	15	46
	Breathing-pause with raising of heels, lifting of arms, deep knee-bending .			12	12	
3	Raising of trunk from recumbent position, back of head on floor	12		40	35	48
	Breathing-pause with raising of heels and deep knee-bending . . .			12	12	
4	Twisting of trunk right round with "side-bending," standing	10		32	28	50
	Breathing - pause with raising of heels and deep knee-bending . .			12	12	
5	Circling of arms, with weight thrown forward on one leg	2 × 16	According to capacity and inclination.	18	15	52
	Breathing-pause with raising of heels and deep knee-bending . . .			12	12	
6	Circling of legs, lying down . .	2 × 8		35	60	54
	Breathing - pause with raising of heels, lifting of arms, and deep knee-bending			12	12	
7	"Forward leaning" to the sides, with trunk twisted, standing . . .	10		30	22	56
	Breathing - pause with raising of heels and deep knee-bending . .			12	12	
8	Bending and straightening of arms, face downwards, weight resting on hands and toes	12		30	40	58
	Threefold pause for breathing, undressing, and preparing bath [2] . .			36	36	
	Bath			105	105	58
	Thorough drying of body . .			115	115	60
9	Rubbing of feet, top of the back, and the neck	2 × 25		18	15	64
	Seconds . . .			598	595	

[1] Delicate people and beginners should omit the knee-bending, and perhaps also the raising of the heels. (See p. 42.)

[2] Delicate people and beginners should make this pause long enough for the pulse to become normal again, but not long enough for them to get cold.

134

TIME-TABLE.

No. of Ex.	Name of Exercise.	Number of times repeated.	Time in seconds.			Explained on p.
			For Beginners.	Those more advanced.	Those in good practice.	
	Carried forward . .			598	595	
10	Rubbing of arms, shoulders, and round armpits, together with deep knee-bendings without raising heels . .	10		20	25	66
	Short breathing-pause, lifting of arms and heels			6	6	
11	Bending of trunk (backwards and forwards) with abdominal movements and rubbing lengthways of front and back of body	20		45	35	68
	Breathing-pause with raising of heels, lifting of arms, and deep knee-bending			12	12	
12	Side-leaning of body with bending of knee and rubbing of thighs and hips and horizontal rubbing of stomach and diaphragm	16		30	35	70
	Breathing-pause with raising of heels, lifting of arms, and deep knee-bending			12	12	
13	Twisting of trunk half round with swinging of arms, downward pressure and rubbing of back	16		36	38	70
	Short breathing-pause with lifting of arms and raising of heels . . .			6	6	
14	Raising of each leg in turn, sideways, with rubbing of hips and thighs . .	20		25	30	72
	Short breathing-pause with lifting of arms and raising of heels . . .			6	6	
15	Raising of each knee in turn with upward rubbing of sides of legs and front of body and downward rubbing of the back	16		38	40	76
	Breathing-pause with raising of heels, lifting of arms, and deep knee-bending			12	12	
16	Flinging of trunk to the sides and rubbing of sides of body . . .	20		8	6	76
	Breathing-pause with raising of heels, lifting of arms, and deep knee-bending			12	12	
17	Flinging twists of trunk and rubbing across the breast	20		12	10	78
	Breathing-pause with raising of heels, lifting of arms, and deep knee-bending			12	12	
18	Flinging of trunk backwards and forwards and rubbing of back and front .	20		10	8	80
	Seconds			900	900	

(Column: According to capacity and inclination.)

= 15 minutes.

135

Printed in Great Britain
by Amazon